SUGAR ORCHIDS
for Cakes

SUGAR **ORCHIDS**

for Cakes

ALAN DUNN, TONY WARREN, TOMBI PECK

MEREHURST

Contents

Introduction

After our successful collaboration on *Sugar Roses for Cakes*, we decided the natural progression was to write a book on orchids, as they are such a fascinating family of plants. We have had to choose only a few examples of orchids for this book; some are our favourites, and others have been included as they are suitable for cakes.

Orchids are thought to have originated during the early Cretaceous period, some 120 million years ago, on the original great land mass of Pangaea. At that time the first orchids existed, possibly occupying an area that is now Malaysia. As the plates of the continents slowly separated, so the orchids moved with them and became dispersed around the world. One of the orchids which was once widespread across this ancient landmass was vanilla, whose pods are still used for flavouring.

Opinions differ as to just how many species the orchid family includes; it has been suggested that it may vary between 14,000 and 35,000. How many of those are natural-growing orchids is not known: estimates suggest the number of naturally occurring species is over 25,000 with new species still being discovered. Today, orchids are divided into approximately 750 separate genera.

Orchids may be terrestrial or epiphytic in their growth. The terrestrial orchids grow on the ground, mostly in forest or woodland leaf litter and in grassland over a wide area; but they also occur on almost any terrain from deserts to semi-aquatic. In Arctic Russia, species of *Cypripedium* flourish under the snow, the flowers appearing as the snow recedes in the spring. Even more extraordinary are the two Australian species of *Rhizanthella* only discovered in 1928 by a farmer ploughing his fields. These orchids are completely subterranean, growing and flowering entirely under the ground. Today, orchids colonize almost every part of the world, continually adapting and evolving into the huge multi-formed and highly successful family of plants called Orchidaceae.

The first known references to orchids are found in Eastern literature in the writings of Confucius, a Chinese sage born in 551BC. The Greek philosopher Theophrastus (c. 372-287 BC), a pupil of Aristotle, first used the word *orchis* to classify this fascinating, diverse family of plants. He is sometimes called the father of botany. In his manuscript *Enquiry into Plants*, *orchis* (meaning testis) referred to the underground tuberous roots of the Mediterranean orchids.

The first reference to orchids in the Western hemisphere is in the *Badianus Codex*, an Aztec herbal of 1552. It depicts vanilla as being used as a flavouring, as a perfume and in the making of a concoction called tlilxochitl, a lotion for health.

The earliest tropical orchid from the New World to flower in England (in 1731) arrived as a 'dried' herbarium specimen. It had sprouted from the seemingly lifeless 'bulb' during its transit from Jamaica and, when potted up, grew and flowered. This plant is *Bletia verrucunda*.

It was not until the eighteenth century that botanical science was born and the first attempts at classification were made. The great Swedish botanist Carolus Linnaeus introduced systematic botany with his *Genera Plantarum*, published in 1737.

Warren, Peck 'n' Dunn

Bibliography

The Orchid by P. Francis Hunt
Orchids – The Royal Horticultural Society by Wilma and Brian Ritterhausen
Orchids by Peter McKenzie Black
The Conservation International Book of Orchids by Jack Kramer

Equipment and Techniques

This section contains a list of the basic equipment and techniques required to make the sugar flowers and foliage featured in the book. Special pieces of equipment for specific cakes or flowers are listed with each set of instructions. Most of the equipment is available from specialist cake decoration suppliers.

EQUIPMENT

Board and Rolling Pin

A non-stick board and rolling pin are essential for rolling out flowerpaste. A dark green non-stick board can be preferable to a white board, which tends to strain the eyes. You may also prefer to use a grooved board to make thick central ridges on petals and leaves.

Celsticks

Available in four sizes: small, medium, large and extra large. One end of each tool is pointed and the other is rounded. The pointed end is used to open up the centres of flowers and can also be used for veining. The rounded end is used rather like a dog bone tool, and has the advantage of a range of different sized tools for the various sizes of flowers and leaves. The central part of each of the celsticks can also be used as a rolling pin for flowers formed from a pedestal shape. They are also used for rolling thick ridges on paste, needed for wired petals and leaves.

Ceramic Silk Veining Tool and Smooth Ceramic Tool (HP)

The silk veining tool has veins on the surface; when rolled over the paste it gives a delicate texture. It can also frill the edges of petals, veining them at

the same time. The smooth ceramic tool is similar in shape to the veining tool but has no markings on it. It is very useful for curling rose petals.

Column Moulds

Hawthorn Hill produce a number of orchid cutters/veiners. The column moulds are particularly useful as they enable you to produce a great number of columns the same size. Then, by altering the resulting columns slightly, a wide range of variations can be produced.

Cutters

There are many different types of cutters available. Cutters speed up the flower-making process and lend consistency and accuracy to your work. Metal cutters come in a greater variety of shapes and can be adjusted

by bending. Plastic cutters are ideal for the intricate working involved in foliage. Most cutters used in this book are readily available from good cake decorating shops, though some will need to be ordered.

Dresden/Veining Tool

The black dresden/veining tool made by Jem is particularly good. The fine end is used for drawing veins down the centre of petals, sepals and leaves. The broad end is used to draw veins and to hollow out the edges and centres of petals and leaves. It can also be used to create an effect known as 'double frilling'. This gives a 'serrated' look and is ideal for creating jagged or ragged edges to both leaves and petals.

Floristry Tape

Paper floristry tape is available in many colours, but the most commonly used are nile green, dark green, white, beige, twig and brown. The tape has a glue in it that is released when the paper is stretched, so it is important to stretch the tape firmly as you tape over a wire.

Florists' Staysoft

This is a form of plasticine, sold in blocks by florists' suppliers and some cake decorating shops and art shops.

Arranging flowers in staysoft allows them to be removed and re-arranged if necessary. A container or disc must be used so that it does not come into contact with the cake.

Foam Pads

These are used to hold paste while you soften or vein a petal or leaf. There are several commercially available pads. Dimpled foam is very useful for shaping petals and leaves while drying,

Great Impressions (GI) Veiners

These are double-sided rubber veiners moulded from real flowers and foliage. They add realism to flower work. Once you have cut out the leaf or petal and inserted a wire, place the shape into the veiner (the ridge on the paste should fit into the back piece of the veiner). Press the two sides together firmly and then remove the leaf, now veined on both sides to a natural finish. You will need to assess the thickness of paste required for some of the more heavily veined petals and leaves – if you make the paste too fine, the veiner may cut through it!

Metal Ball Tools

Metal ball tools are intended for use with cold porcelain, but they work equally well on sugar. More comfortable than plastic dog bone tools, they can be used in exactly the same way but if rolled, rather than dragged, along the edge of a petal a more beautiful fluting is achieved.

Needle Frilling Tool

Used to soften the edges of petals, this tool creates a completely different look to that achieved with a dog bone or a ball tool. A cocktail or saté stick (toothpick) can also be used, but the metal tool is much kinder to the fingers.

Non-toxic Glue Stick

This is a basic glue stick available in most stationery shops and is used for fixing ribbons to cake boards.

Non-toxic Hi-tack Glue (Impex)

This is a non-toxic glue used to glue stamens onto wire. It is safe to use on flowers with wires in them but should not come into immediate contact with cake surfaces. Note that this type of glue is not permissible for use on competition work.

Paintbrushes

Good brushes are one of the most important items in a flower-maker's kit. Remember that the final control and accuracy with colouring can make or break your work. Flat brushes are the most useful for dusting flowers and foliage (round brushes are not firm enough to colour accurately with dusting powders). Brushes by Robert Simmons called Craft Painters Nos 6 and 8 are particularly recommended, along with their Shaders. You will need a good selection of finer brushes for painting fine details on flowers and foliage. We find that it is preferable to use a different brush for each main colour in order to avoid the problem of dirty colouring.

Plain Edge Cutting Wheel (PME)

A 'must have' for any sugarcrafter's workbox. This tool enables you to cut pastillage or flowerpaste without any 'pulling' and gives very good control when you are cutting out leaves and petals freehand.

Pliers and Wire Cutters

Small, fine-nosed pliers are essential. They can be purchased from electrical supply shops, or in the jewellery sections of craft shops. Wire cutters are also very useful: either electrical cutters or heavy duty florists' scissors.

Silicone Plastique (CS)

Food grade silicone plastique is a base material (white) mixed with a catalyst (blue). Mix equal amounts of the two materials together, no more than you need to create one side of a veiner. You have between 10 and 30 minutes before it sets, depending on the room temperature. Roll a ball of paste, smooth it against plastic sheet and press the raised veins (usually the

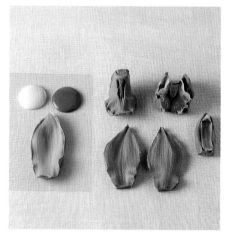

back of a leaf or petal) against the material, gradually removing air bubbles. Allow to set. Remove the leaf/petal. Coat with white fat or cold cream, being careful not to leave any in the veins. Mix up more silicone and press onto the first part. Allow to set. Gently prise the two veiners apart.

Stamens

There is a vast range of stamens available to the flower-maker. You may prefer to use mainly white stamens and colour them the required colour with petal dust. Keep a supply of small white seedhead stamens and some finer white stamens, as well as both large and small lily stamens, to hand.

Tape Shredder

This is used to cut lengths of floristry tape into various widths. If you remove one of the blades, you will

have a shredder that will cut one half- and two quarter-width lengths at the same time. The blades are actually razor blades and will need to be replaced occasionally and cleaned regularly.

Wires

The quality of the wires available varies; the best wire available for sugarcrafters is Sunrise wire. If this cannot be obtained, then it is best to buy A-grade wire, which can be identified by a red spot on the packet. You may prefer to buy white wire in gauges from 33-gauge (fine) to 24-gauge (thicker) and then tape over the wire with nile green floristry tape during the assembly of the flower. There are also stronger wires available from 22-gauge to 14-gauge (the higher the number, the finer the wire). These can be covered or uncovered

and it doesn't matter which you use. You can also buy very fine silk-covered 36-gauge wire on a reel, which is ideal for very small flowers.

TECHNIQUES

Wiring Leaves and Petals

There are many ways to wire leaves and petals. There are two main methods used throughout this book. Method 1: Roll out flowerpaste to the required thickness, leaving a thick ridge down the centre – this can be achieved by rolling a piece of well kneaded paste with small rolling pin, manipulating the paste to leave a thick ridge at the centre for a wire. Cut out the petal or leaf shape, lining the thick ridge down the centre of the cutter. Press the cutter down firmly, then release the paste from the cutter. Moisten the end of a wire and insert it into the thick ridge, holding the leaf firmly between your finger and thumb to prevent the wire from piercing through the paste. Always insert the wire into at least half the length of the paste ridge to ensure support. Method 2: Roll out flowerpaste over a grooved board. Moisten the wire and stick it on the paste over the groove line. Fold back the paste and then re-roll to sandwich the wire. Cut out the leaf/petal and work as required.

Colouring

A limited selection of paste or liquid food colourings is required. Petal dust, or dusting powder, may also be used to colour the paste, but are usually used for colouring after shaping. If you decide to mix powders into flower-paste as colouring, avoid large amounts as they can alter the consistency. You may find it preferable to colour the paste a paler tone of the

colour you want the finished flower to be, then dust on top to achieve greater depth.

It is important to have a good selection of petal dust colours and to experiment with different colour combinations to obtain the effect you want. The colours can either be mixed together or simply brushed onto the paste in layers. The instructions for each of the flowers in this book include a list of colours used. It is better to mix up a large pot of colour in advance, rather than mixing up small amounts at a time, as this wastes both time and petal dust. If you want to make a colour paler, it will need to be mixed with white petal dust.

Sometimes a little cornflour is used to clean the colour out of a brush and to give a very subtle tinge to the petal tips. You may need to use a few liquid colours, the main ones being cyclamen and holly berry, to paint detail spots and lines onto petals.

Glazing

There are several ways to add a glaze to flowers and leaves. The steaming method is used not to give a high gloss, but rather to create a 'waxy' finish or, more often, to remove the dry dusted appearance left by petal dust. It is also used when trying to create a velvety finish or for darkening the depth of colour on a flower or a leaf, since the surface of the paste is still slightly damp after steaming. Hold each flower or leaf in the steam from a boiling kettle for a few seconds, or until the surface turns shiny. Take care, as too much steam can soften the sugar and cause it to dissolve.

For a more permanent and shiny glaze, use confectioners' varnish. Used neat (full glaze), this gives a high gloss ideal for berries and glossy leaves. For most foliage this looks too artificial, so it is better to dilute the varnish with isopropyl alcohol (available from sugarcraft shops, where it is usually called 'dipping alcohol'). Mix the varnish and alcohol in a lidded container and shake to mix – not too much as this will create tiny air bubbles. The glaze can be used straight away; simply dip the leaf, petal or a group of pieces into the glaze, shake off the excess and dry on absorbent kitchen paper. The glaze may be applied with a paintbrush, but the brush strokes tend to remove the colour in streaks and unless the brush is very carefully cleaned afterwards, it will be ruined.

The following glazes are those most often used:

Three-quarters Glaze
Quarter part alcohol to three-quarters varnish. This gives a semi-gloss without the 'plastic' appearance of a full glaze.

Half Glaze
Equal proportions of alcohol and varnish. This gives a natural shine that is ideal for many types of foliage, including ivy and rose leaves.

Quarter Glaze
Three-quarters alcohol to a quarter part varnish. This is used for leaves that don't have much shine; the glaze just takes away the flat, dusty look of a leaf or petal.

Using a 'Cage'
A wire 'cage' is used to mark the impression of unopened petals on a bud. The 'cage' is made from wire, the gauge depending on the size of the bud. If you are making the bud of a five-petalled flower, you will need five pieces of wire for the 'cage'. Tape the pieces of wire together at one end with half width floristry tape. Bend the taped section of wire in half and tape over this again; it will prevent wires being pulled loose during the marking of the bud. Open up the cage, trying not to cross the wires at the base. Insert the modelled bud, tip or base first, depending on the effect required. Close the wires onto its surface, keeping them as evenly spaced as possible. For some buds, a more realistic effect is achieved if the paste between the wires is pinched out and thinned with your finger and thumb to form a ridge that gives the appearance of larger petals. After removing from the 'cage', twist to give a spiral effect.

Flowerpaste
The type of flowerpaste (gum paste) you use is a matter of personal preference. A paste that stretches well and does not dry out on the surface too quickly will allow you to wire petals together while they are still damp (a factor that most pastes fail to achieve). Ready-made

flowerpaste (by mail order) tends to be more consistent than homemade paste, and will save you a lot of time and trouble. Make your own from the following recipe if you wish.

25ml (5 teaspoons) cold water
10ml (2 teaspoons) powdered gelatine
500g (1lb 2oz/4 cups) icing (confectioners') sugar, sifted
15ml (3 teaspoons) gum tragacanth
10ml (2 teaspoons) liquid glucose
15ml (3 teaspoons) white vegetable fat (shortening)
1 medium egg white

1 Mix the water and gelatine together in a small heatproof bowl and leave to stand for 30 minutes. Sift the icing sugar and gum tragacanth into the bowl of a heavy-duty mixer and mix.

2 Place the bowl with the gelatine mixture over a saucepan of hot water and stir until the gelatine has dissolved. Warm a teaspoon in hot water, then measure out the liquid glucose (the heat should help to ease the glucose off the spoon).

3 Add the glucose and white fat to the gelatine mixture, and continue to heat until all of the ingredients have melted and are thoroughly mixed together. Add the dissolved gelatine mixture to the icing sugar, along with the egg white. Fit the beater to the machine and turn it on at its lowest speed. Beat until mixed, then increase the speed to maximum until the paste becomes white and stringy.

4 Remove the flowerpaste from the bowl and rub a thin layer of white fat over it to prevent the outer part from drying out. Place in a plastic bag and store in an airtight container. Allow the flowerpaste to rest and to mature for at least 12 hours before using it.

Working with Flowerpaste

You will need a pot of fresh egg white, a pot of cornflour or cornflour bag and white vegetable fat (shortening). The continued use of fresh egg white is far superior to any

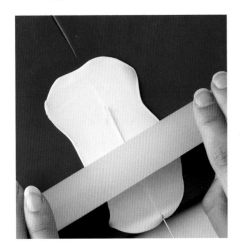

other substitutes. However, if you are doubtful about using egg white you may choose to use edible glue instead.

The paste should be kneaded well before it is modelled into a flower or rolled out on a board, otherwise it has a tendency to dry out and crack around the edges. If the paste is dry or tough, soften it using fresh egg white (not gum arabic etc) – do not add in large quantities as this makes the paste short and difficult to work with, plus it will take longer to dry.

If the paste is sticky, then a small amount of white fat may be used on the fingers while you knead it – but do not add too much! For many people, there is a temptation to add cornflour to the paste when it is sticky. Cornflour can be used on the surface of the paste quite happily.

Always grease the board with white fat, then remove almost completely with absorbent kitchen paper. This will form a very thin layer of fat on the board and stop the paste gripping to the board. If you use too much fat it will show up on the finished petal or leaf when you apply dusting powder.

Although commercial paste does not tend to dry out very quickly, it is advisable if you are cutting out a large number of petals to cover them with a celflap or a plastic bag to prevent the surface crusting over.

Coating with Sugarpaste

1 Knead the sugarpaste (cold rolled fondant) to make it smooth; try not to knead too many air bubbles into it. Lightly dust the work surface with icing (confectioners') sugar. Roll out the sugarpaste to an even thickness, about 1cm (½in). Moisten the surface of the almond paste with clear alcohol (Kirsch or Cointreau). Form an even coating of alcohol – if you have dry areas, these will be prone to forming air bubbles with the sugarpaste.

2 Lift the sugarpaste over the cake and ease it into position, smoothing out the top. Trim the sugarpaste from around the base of the cake. Polish the top and the sides using sugarpaste smoothers. You can also use a pad of sugarpaste pressed into the palm of your hand to smooth the edges and corners of the cake. If you catch the paste and make an indent, try smoothing it over with the pad of sugarpaste.

Cold Porcelain

Care must be taken to work in a well ventilated area when making cold porcelain. Homemade cold porcelain

must never be placed in contact with a food product and must not be used as an alternative to flowerpaste for cake decoration. We recommend its use for non-edible items such as floral arrangements, plants in candle holders, corsages, bouquets, etc.

30–45ml (2–3 tablespoons) baby oil
125ml (4fl oz/½cup) non-toxic hi-tack glue (Impex)
125ml (4fl oz/½cup) white PVA woodglue
100g (4oz/1cup) cornflour
Permanent white gouache

1 Measure the oil into a medium-sized non-stick pan and add the glue. Stir them together to a thick cream. Add 1 cup of cornflour and stir it in. Place over medium heat until the paste has collected around the spoon as for choux pastry. Scrape any uncooked paste from the spoon as you are cooking. The paste should feel spongy to the touch.

2 Turn the paste onto a non-stick board. Cover with clingfilm and allow to cool for a few minutes. Like bread dough, the paste will cling to your fingers at the beginning. Resist adding extra cornflour unless there is no sign that it is coming off your fingers. Do not add more than an extra 25g (1oz/¼cup) as it is difficult to soften the paste again. A softer paste is best which will stiffen as you work it.

3 Add permanent white gouache to the paste to prevent yellowing and extreme translucence. Wrap the paste in clingfilm, place it in a plastic bag and store in an airtight container. Do not place in a refrigerator as the cold will break down the glue!

Springtime Wedding

I designed this wedding cake to display on the Table of Honour at the British Sugarcraft Guild's International Exhibition 2001. Cream *Cymbidium* orchids, burgundy curly *Dendrobium* orchids and ribbon fern have been used creatively to give this cake a lively spring feeling.
Tony

Cake and decoration

15cm (6in), 20cm (8in) and 25cm (10in) oval cakes

1.75kg (4lb) white almond paste

2.5kg (5½lb) white sugarpaste

23cm (9in) thin oval cake board

20cm (8in) and 33cm (13in) oval boards

1.35m (1½yd) burgundy lady chiffon ribbon

White ribbon to trim board

No. 0 piping tube (tip)

Scroll cutter (FMM)

Shimmer pink lustre colour

10 stems of curly dendrobium orchids

16 sets of ribbon fern leaves

6 burgundy wire loops

2 small cymbidium orchids (p 20)

Preparation

1 Brush the cakes with apricot glaze, cover with almond paste, then leave to dry. Moisten the surface of the almond paste with clear alcohol and cover with white sugarpaste using smoothers to achieve a good finish.

2 Place the 20cm (8in) oval cake onto the 23cm (9in) thin cake board.

3 Cover the two remaining cake boards with white sugarpaste and position a cake on top, making sure it is central and that there is a neat join between the cake base and board. Leave to dry for a few days.

4 Place the 20cm (8in) cake on top of the 25cm (10in) cake, towards the right hand side.

5 Using royal icing, secure a band of burgundy chiffon ribbon around each of the cakes. Pipe a floral design on the side of the ribbon using the No. 0 piping tube (tip) and white royal icing. Trim the boards with white ribbon.

Side design

6 Roll out a little white sugarpaste and, using a scroll cutter, cut out several scrolls. Secure these to the edge of the cakes. Dust each scroll with shimmer pink lustre colour.

Assembly

7 Make up two sprays by taping together five stems of dendrobium orchids to the fern leaves. Tape a cymbidium orchid (template page 152) to three stems of fern leaves, then tape the five stems of dendrobium orchids and fern to the main stem. Cut three burgundy colour wires into three different lengths, taping them into loops and attaching them to the back of the spray.

8 Place each of the sprays into a posy pick and insert one into the large cake and the other into the small cake. It is important to leave the top of the posy pick showing so it can be seen when the cake is cut.

9 Place a band of burgundy ribbon around the outside of an 8cm (3in) x 4cm (1½in) separator plate and secure with tape. Place the separator plate on top of the middle tier and position the small cake on top.

Curly dendrobium orchid

The *Dendrobium* genus is considered to be the second largest of the orchid family, consisting of about 1,000 distinct known species. This unusual curly orchid is a hybrid form of one of the Australian orchids. The petals are very fragile, so it is important to allow them to breathe, giving them plenty of space in an arrangement or bouquet.

Materials

Pale melon flowerpaste
20- and 26-gauge white wires
White, primrose, violet and aubergine petal dusts
Nile green floristry tape

Equipment

Curly dendrobium orchid cutters (TT 843–845) or template (p 152)
Dendrobium veiners made from silicone plastique, p 8 (CS)

Column

1 Roll a small piece of pale melon paste into a ball and place into the column mould to form the column. Remove from the mould and insert a moistened, hooked 26-gauge white wire into the back of the column.

Labellum (lip/throat)

2 Roll out a piece of flowerpaste and cut out the lip using the lip cutter, then place into the lip veiner to vein.

Remove from the veiner and soften the two round edges with a metal ball tool. Flute the bottom edge with a dresden tool.

3 Moisten the V of the lip with a little egg white and secure to the tail of the column, then leave to dry.

Sepals and petals

4 Roll out a piece of flowerpaste and cut out the three sepals. These sepals

are all cut out using one cutter at the same time.

5 Roll out a further piece of flowerpaste and cut out the two long petals (wing petals). Shape using the single sepal cutter.

6 Place the sepals and petals in their appropriate veiners to vein. Remove from the veiner. Place on a pad and gently frill the edges.

7 Gently spiral the single wing petals and place on dimpled foam to dry off a little as they will then hold their shape better.

8 Attach the petals to the sepals with either glue or softened flowerpaste. Place the petals in between the dorsal and lateral sepals.

9 Moisten the central section below the petals in between the lateral

sepals. Thread the wire with the column and lip through the sepals in the centre of the dorsal and lateral petals. Press the dorsal sepal very firmly against the back of the column to secure.

10 Cut a slot in a small thin piece of foam, then place the stem of the orchid into the slot in dimpled foam to support the sepals and petals until they are completely dry.

Buds

11 Roll a ball of pale melon flowerpaste into a teardrop shape, pinch the tip to a point and curve the teardrop, stroking it at the same time to flatten one side.

12 Pinch a small spur at the base of the bud and shape with your fingers until it is complete. Insert a hooked and moistened 26-gauge wire into the back of the bud at a slight angle,

towards the base, pinching the paste onto the wire to secure.

13 Make a few veins on the bud using a dresden tool, and cut down the side to make it look as if the bud is about to open. Have a specimen flower to hand to copy carefully.

Colouring

14 Thicken each of the buds and flowers with nile green floristry tape.

Mix together white petal dust with a little primrose petal dust, and dust very lightly into the throat of the orchid. Also dust to the side of the labellum onto the lateral petals and sepals.

15 Mix together violet and a little aubergine petal dust and, starting from the tips, dust approximately three-quarters of the way down each of the lateral petals and sepals back and front. Be very careful not to break the two lateral petals, as they are very fragile and easily damaged at this stage.

Assembly

16 Starting with the smaller of the buds, tape them to a 20-gauge wire using half width nile green floristry tape. Continue adding the buds down the stem, leaving the stem longer on each bud as they get bigger.

17 Dust the buds first with pale primrose petal dust and then with a pale mixture of violet and aubergine dusts. The smaller buds should be slightly darker in colour. Add the flowers, leaving a good length of stem for movement.

18 Finally, steam the whole orchid stem to seal the colour and give a realistic slight waxy look to the finished flower.

Pseudobulbs and leaves

19 These dendrobium orchids produce elongated pseudobulbs known as canes which can grow up to 45cm (18in) tall with leaves produced at right angles all along their length. The flowers are produced in groups of two or three along the canes in the spaces between the leaves. See page 142 for instructions on how to produce the pseudobulbs and leaves for this orchid.

Ribbon fern

These popular small ferns may be found in many parts of the world, from tropical rain forest to European woodland. The best known species is *Pteris cretica*, the ribbon fern, which is found growing wild in Italy and many parts of Asia and Africa.

Materials
Mid green flowerpaste
24-, 26- and 28-gauge white wires
Moss green petal dust
Half glaze
Olive green floristry tape
Equipment
Fern cutters (TT 837–842) or templates (p 152)
Fern veiner

1 Roll out the mid green flowerpaste, leaving a ridge down the centre of the paste. Using the fern cutter or the template on page 152, cut out a set of leaves. Be careful as these are fragile. Insert a moistened 26-gauge wire into the larger leaves and a 28-gauge into the smaller ones, then vein.

2 Remove from the veiner and flute down either side of the leaf using a dresden tool. Place on a pad and soften the edges with a metal ball tool. Place to one side to dry.

Colouring and assembly
3 Dust the outer edges and centre veins of the leaves with moss green petal dust. The backs of the leaves are paler in colour. Dip the leaves into half glaze. Tape a 24-gauge wire to the larger centre leaf, then add the two side leaves, remembering to face them the right way.

New Romantic Bouquet

This eye-catching, modern bridal bouquet, with its striking combination of green *Cymbidium* orchids, red roses and pink peppertree berries, could be used as the main feature on a wedding cake. If the flowers were made from cold porcelain, it could be carried as an actual bouquet. Long curving trails of red paper-covered wire have been used to create an unusual twist in the design. *Alan*

Flowers

4 trailing stems of vanilla orchid foliage and 3 pods (p 120)

3 green cymbidium orchids

2 red rosebuds (p 150)

2 full red roses (step 4)

3 half red roses

5 anthurium leaves

Eucalyptus or other suitable foliage

3 stems of peppertree berries, plus four smaller clusters

Materials and equipment

Nile green floristry tape

18-gauge wire

Fine-nosed pliers

Wire cutters or florist's scissors

Red paper-covered florist's wire

Red or green velvet ribbon to trim bouquet handle

Preparation

1 Using half or even full width green tape, tape 18-gauge wire onto any of the flower and foliage stems that need extra support or length. The longest trailing stem should form about two thirds of the total length of bouquet.

Assembly

2 Form the basic outline of the bouquet using the trailing stems of vanilla foliage. Bend each stem to a 90-degree angle and tape together.

3 Create the focal point by adding a cymbidium orchid at the centre – this flower should stand proud. Now add the remaining two orchids to create a line through the bouquet.

4 To achieve depth through the bouquet, add the red roses in a line at a much lower level to the orchids, using the buds at the edges and the larger flowers at the centre. (The red roses were dusted with red, ruby and aubergine petal dusts.) Outline the bouquet with anthurium leaves. Next, add a few stems of eucalyptus foliage and the peppertree berries.

5 Add a few loops of red wire to the bouquet, plus several long lengths of wire tied together with a few clusters of berries wired at intervals down the length. Neaten the handle by wrapping it with green or red velvet ribbon – use glass-headed pins to hold the ribbon at the handle top.

Cymbidium orchid

Cymbidium orchids are one of the most popular in cultivation today. The hybrids form the major part of the collection. Some of the species hold their own amongst the modern hybrids. The genus is very versatile with the plants' varying habitats, and has evolved into many different shapes and forms. The species are found in temperate or tropical parts of northwestern India, China, Japan, through Southeast Asia and Australia. The hybrids have been bred from a handful of species from the Himalayas.

Materials

White and vine green flowerpaste

22- and 24-gauge white wires

Vine green, aubergine, edelweiss, lemon, primrose, moss and foliage petal dusts

Deep magenta craft dust

Cyclamen liquid food colour

Nile green floristry tape

Equipment

Hybrid cymbidium orchid cutters (TT831–834) or templates (p 153)

Homemade cymbidium orchid veiners

Preparation

1 It is not essential to make your own veiners for this flower, but the finished flower will be even more realistic if you do! It is best to take the mould from a mature orchid as the veins of the flower will be much more pronounced. Full instructions on how to make your own veiners/moulds are on page 8. I have made moulds for the column, labellum (lip/throat), lateral petals and sepals.

Column

2 Form a ball of white paste into a long teardrop shape. Lightly dust the column mould with cornflour, then squeeze the flowerpaste into the mould. Hollow out the centre using the rounded end of a large celstick. Trim off any excess paste. Insert a moistened 22-gauge white wire into the base of the column – insert the wire quite a good way up the column to give it support and strength.

3 Add a ball of white paste at the top of the column to represent the anther cap. Using a sharp scalpel, indent the centre of the ball to create a division. Indent the ball at the base to flatten it slightly against the main body of the column. Allow to dry. Dust the back of the column with a light dusting of vine green petal dust, and then deep magenta craft dust with a touch of aubergine petal dust. Dust the anther cap with a mixture of edelweiss, lemon and primrose just to

raised platform at the centre of the throat that hopefully your mould will have picked up. Cut out the labellum petal using either a cutter or the template and a sharp scalpel. Place the petal into the bottom half of the mould and then squeeze the top half on top. As you squeeze the two halves of the mould together you will end up with some excess paste over the edges. Trim off the excess paste. Frill the bottom section of the lip with a silk veining tool. Cup the two

Colouring
5 Dust the edges of the petal with vine green petal dust. Take some of the colour onto the lip and some inside the throat. Dust the raised central platform and a little of the petal around it with a mixture of lemon and primrose petal dusts. It is best to have a real flower or a good photograph to copy the painted markings onto the lip. They can be blotches, stripes or spots (and some varieties have no markings). I have

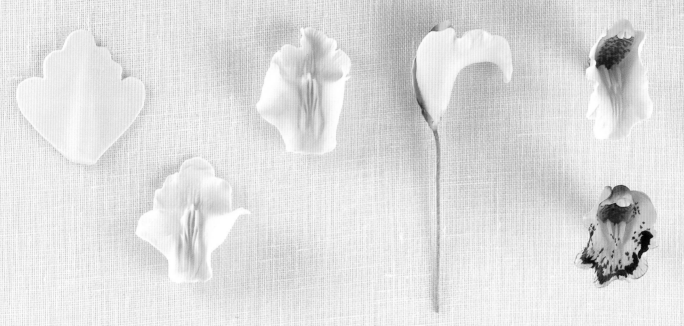

take the starkness off the white paste. Using a fine paintbrush and cyclamen liquid colour, paint lots of spots onto the hollowed underside. Dust over with a little primrose and lemon mixed together.

Labellum (lip/throat)
4 Roll out some vine green paste quite thick, leaving a ridge at the centre. The thickness at the centre of the throat is important as there is a

side sections slightly (some cymbidiums have no cupping at all). Moisten the bottom 'V' shaped edge to the petal and then attach onto the dried column. Reshape the throat as required. You should be able to see most of the back of the column. Allow to dry. If you have made the throat with the cutter and no mould, you will need to add an extra sausage of paste split into two with angled tweezers or a scalpel. Allow to dry.

used cyclamen liquid colour and added spots and blotches onto the lip. Add a few spots to the raised platform too. Dust the very edges of the petal and around the heavy lip markings with magenta dust.

Lateral petals
6 Roll out some more vine green paste to form a fleshy petal, leaving a raised ridge for the wire. Cut out the petal shape using either the cutter or

the template and a sharp scalpel. Insert a moistened 24-gauge white wire into the thick ridge, supporting the ridge either side with your finger and thumb to prevent the wire piercing through the petal. Soften the edge of the petal slightly and then vein using the petal veiner. Pinch the petal from the base to the tip to give the petal a natural shape, but try not to create a very heavy central vein.

the back inside edges with a small ball tool to encourage them to curl back. Allow to rest and firm up slightly over a curve, hollowed side down.

Lateral sepals

8 Repeat as in step 6, using the lateral sepal cutter to create a left and a right sepal. Vein them both using the lateral sepal veiners. Pinch the length of each sepal. There is a

from the base to the tip with vine green and edelweiss mixed together, fading the colour towards the edges. Dust the edges of each petal/sepal with deep magenta craft dust and then overdust with a very light touch of aubergine petal dust. Add a little of the colour to the base of each petal too. Sometimes there are some tiny spots at the base of the petals/sepals as well.

Repeat to make a left and a right hand petal.

Dorsal sepal

7 Roll out and cut out the sepal as described in step 6, but using the dorsal sepal cutter/template. Vein the sepal using the dorsal sepal veiner. Pinch from the base to the tip to give added shape. As you handle the petal, try to hollow it out slightly with your fingers. Carefully work the petal on

curved lift at the base of each lateral sepal – try to encourage the paste into shape using your fingers. Allow to rest curling back over a former.

Colouring and assembly

9 It is best to not allow the petals/sepals to dry completely before you dust and wire the flower together. A more realistic shape may be achieved if the paste is malleable. Dust each petal/sepal on the back and front

10 Tape the lateral petals onto either side of the labellum/column using half width nile green floristry tape. Next, add the dorsal and lateral sepals behind the petals. Reshape the flower if the paste is still wet. Allow to dry.

11 Set the colour of the orchid by holding it over a jet of steam – this will give it a little sheen. Do not give the flower too much of a glaze.

Peppertree/Anthurium

These pretty berries (*Schinus molle*) are from the South American pepper tree. In Peru, a mildly alcoholic drink is made from the ground down seeds of the tree. The seeds are also used as a condiment and an adulterant for pepper. The tree itself is a good source of tannin that is used in the leather industry. They are also used by florists in bouquets and arrangements. The bold foliage pictured here are *Anthurium* leaves. These were used with the berries in the New Romantic Bouquet.

Materials
24- and 33-gauge white wires
Very pale green flowerpaste
Ruby, aubergine, foliage green and nutkin brown petal dusts
Full glaze
Nile green floristry tape

1 Cut lots of short lengths of 33-gauge wire. Bend a tiny hook in the end of each. Roll a small ball of very pale green paste and insert the moistened hook. Texture the surface slightly by indenting with the rounded end of a paintbrush or ceramic tool.

2 Dust to different degrees with ruby, aubergine and a touch of foliage. Dip into full glaze. Allow to dry.

3 Tape the berries into small groups with quarter width tape. Form longer groups taped onto 24-gauge wire. Dust over the wires and main stem with a mix of aubergine and nutkin brown petal dusts.

Anthurium foliage (above)
Roll out mid green paste quite thickly, with a central thicker section. Insert a 22- or 20-gauge wire into the ridge. Vein in an anthurium veiner (GI), trim and soften the edges. Pinch from base to tip. Dust with forest and foliage, with aubergine at the centre and edge. Dry, then dip in half glaze.

Star of Bethlehem

These amazing, slender-petalled white star of Bethlehem (*Angraecum leonis*) orchids blend beautifully with the silver sage leaves. I have placed the arrangement into a tall vase to show off their long spurs. The painting of the moth is to show how the orchid is pollinated as this is quite a spectacular sight. *Tony*

Preparation

1 Brush the cake with apricot glaze and cover with almond paste. Leave to dry. Moisten the surface of the almond paste with clear alcohol and cover with sugarpaste using smoothers for a good finish.

2 Cover the board with sugarpaste and position the cake centrally on top, making sure that there is a neat join between the cake base and board.

3 Attach a narrow band of ribbon to the base of the cake using a tiny amount of royal icing. Secure a band of ribbon to the edge of the board using double-sided sticky tape.

Cake top design

4 Either paint the design freehand, or use the template supplied on page 153. Mix spruce green paste colour with a little white petal dust and dilute with a small amount of isopropyl alcohol to paint the stem of the orchid and bud. Next, using a clean No. 0 brush, mix white petal dust with a small amount of isopropyl alcohol and paint the orchid and bud, adding a little pale green to the bud and the spurs on both. Using a No.

00 paintbrush, outline the orchid with black paste colour dilute with a small amount of isopropyl alcohol.

5 It may help to find a good picture of a hawk moth to match the colours. Starting with caramel (ivory) paste colour diluted with a small amount of isopropyl alcohol, paint in the background colour, adding the darker paste colours to create a moth.

Assembly

6 Place the cake onto the tilting cake stand. Tape two or three stems of sage leaves to one or two orchids and a bud in various sizes, having some taller than others.

7 Tape two shorter stem of orchids and leaves to the left hand side of the main stem, bending them so they will trail over the cake, and one to the right. Bend a further stem to an angle of 90 degrees and tape to the main stem to trail down the front of the cake. Place the spray into the vase and arrange accordingly. Tape a further stem of three orchids and buds to three stems of sage leaves and arrange carefully at the base of the cake.

Cake and decoration

20cm (8in) teardrop cake
675g (1½lb) white almond paste
1kg (2¼lb) white sugarpaste
25cm (10in) teardrop cake board
3mm and 5mm white ribbon
Spruce green, black, caramel, chestnut brown and dark brown paste colours
White petal dust

Flowers

9 angraecum orchids
5 angraecum orchid buds
12 stems of sage leaves

Equipment

Nos. 00 and 0 synthetic paintbrushes
Small tilting perspex stand
Thin stem vase about 23cm (9in) high

Angraecum orchid

This orchid (*Angraecum leonis*) is centred in Africa, spreading to Madagascar and the Mascarene Islands. Charles Darwin made his famous prediction of the existence of a moth not yet discovered, with the 30cm (12in) proboscis necessary to get to the base of this long spur. It was ultimately found and aptly named *Xanthopan morganii praedicta*. As this orchid is largely moth pollinated, it is night fragrant.

Materials

White, mid green and pale cream flowerpaste

20-, 24- and 26-gauge wires

White bridal satin dust

Vine green petal dust

Moss green, foliage green, champagne and cream petal dusts

Nile green floristry tape

Equipment

Angraecum cutters (TT 225, 850, 851) or templates (p 153)

Stargazer (B) veiner (GI)

Plain edge cutting wheel (PME)

Long leaf veiner

Column

1 Roll a thin length of flowerpaste approximately 13cm (5in) long to form the spur, leaving it thicker at one end. Bend a hook in a half length 24-gauge wire.

2 Moisten a 24-gauge hooked wire and insert into the thicker end of the column, approximately 1cm (½in) down from the top. Turn the column over and, using a dresden tool, slightly

hollow out the underside of the column. Mark a small anther cap to the tip of the column.

Labellum (lip/throat)

3 Take a piece of white flowerpaste and roll out quite thinly. Cut out a lip shape petal using the lip cutter or the template. Place it on a pad and soften the edges using a metal ball tool. Place the petal in the veiner and vein. Remove from the veiner and pinch a ridge from the pointed end of the lip up the centre.

4 Moisten the rounded end of the petal and fix it securely to the column. Leave to dry completely. You may need to support this on a piece of foam.

Dorsal and lateral sepals

5 Roll out white flowerpaste over a grooved board. Place a 26-gauge wire on top of the paste over the groove and bringing the paste back over, sandwiching the wire between the layers of paste.

6 Cut out one dorsal and two lateral sepals, using the sepal cutter or template on page 153. Place on a pad and soften the edges, then vein using the veiner. Place the sepals on dimpled foam and leave them to dry completely.

Petals

7 Repeat step 5, cutting out two petals. Soften the edges and vein as before. Place on dimpled foam to dry.

Colouring

8 Dust the labellum with white bridal satin dust. Add a little vine green petal dust to the tip of the labellum and into the throat and also dust the back of the lip.

9 Dust the top of the column and the long spur with bridal satin and a little vine green.

10 Dust the dorsal, lateral and petals with white bridal satin and a small amount of vine green to the base of each of the petals.

Assembly

11 Tape the two wing petals to either side of the column – these are

the shorter of the petals. Add the shorter head and the longer legs to the stem, taping two or three 20-gauge wires to the stem to strengthen them. Be very careful at this stage not to break off the spur as it is fragile.

Buds

12 Roll a ball of white flowerpaste into a slender teardrop approximately 5cm (2in) long to form the spur. Bend

the thinner end over slightly and flatten on the outer side. Insert a moistened and hooked 24-gauge wire into the flattened side of the spur, and shape the thicker end to a sharp point.

13 Roll a piece of white flowerpaste and, using the smaller petal cutter, cut out three petals. Soften the edges of the petals, then place them in the veiner to vein.

14 Moisten the inside of the petals and arrange around the bud with two petals to the bottom and one to the top. Dust the bud with vine green and then overdust with moss green.

Leaves

15 Roll out a long strip of mid green paste, leaving a thick ridge in the centre. Cut out and insert a moistened 20-gauge white wire. Place

in the veiner, remove and pinch a central ridge. Roll a further long strip of paste, without a ridge. Cut out the leaf and vein. Pinch a vein down the leaf. Moisten the inside of the leaf 4cm (1½in) up from the base. Wrap the leaf around the wired leaf, with the unwired leaf on top. Make as many as required. Add aerial roots using pale cream paste. Dust the leaves with foliage and moss, and the roots with champagne and cream.

Sage

Sage (*Salvia officinalis*) is a well known and very decorative herb. There are several coloured leaf varieties which make excellent plants for flower arrangements. The variety I have chosen to use has beautiful silver foliage.

Materials
Pale eucalyptus and spruce green flowerpaste mixed
22-, 28- and 30-gauge white wires
Moss green, eucalyptus and white petal dusts
Olive green floristry tape

Equipment
Sage leaf cutters (TT 852–855) or templates (p 153)
Sage leaf veiner

Leaves
1 Roll out green flowerpaste, leaving a small ridge in the centre. Cut out the sage leaves in pairs and in various sizes.

2 Insert a moisten 28- or 30-gauge white wire, depending on the size of leaf you are using, soften the edges and position in the veiner to vein. Remove from the veiner and place on foam to dry.

Colouring and assembly
3 Mix moss green with eucalyptus petal dust and dust each of the leaves. Overdust with white petal dust to give a velvety appearance.

4 Tape each leaf stem with green tape, then tape two small leaves onto a 22-gauge wire, leaving the stem of the leaves 1cm (½in) before it is attached to the stem. Continue adding the leaves in pairs, graduating in size.

Madam Butterfly

The *Papilionanthe* orchid is the inspiration for this cake, spotted on a visit to the orchid gardens in the Singapore botanical gardens. The gardens are an orchid enthusiast's delight – I have never seen so many orchid plants in flower *en masse* before. The *Papilionanthe* is the national flower of Singapore, so it was an obvious subject for my design. *Alan*

Cake and decoration

15cm (6in) and 25cm (10in) round cakes
15cm (6in) round thin cake board
1.75kg (3¾lb) white almond paste
2.5kg (5½lb) pale green sugarpaste
38cm (15in) round cake board
Fine and broad magenta ribbon to trim cakes and board
Small amount of white flowerpaste
Myrtle and bridal satin dusts
Plum petal dust

Flowers

7 papilionanthe orchids and 10 buds
About 70 papilionanthe leaves

Equipment

Tiny butterfly cutter/veiner (HH)
3 slim posy picks

Preparation

1 Place the small cake onto the thin cake board, and then brush both cakes with apricot glaze. Cover both cakes with almond paste. Allow to dry. Meanwhile, colour the sugarpaste a pale green (using a small amount of mint green paste food colour). Moisten the almond paste with clear alcohol, then cover both cakes with pale green sugarpaste. Use smoothers to create a neat finish.

2 Cover the cake board with green sugarpaste and then position the large cake on top. Use a sugarpaste smoother again to neaten. Next, position the small cake on top of the large one.

3 Attach a band of magenta ribbon to the base of each cake using either royal icing or some sugarpaste softened with clear alcohol. Glue the broad magenta ribbon to the edge of the cake board using a glue stick.

Side design

4 Roll out a small amount of white flowerpaste and cut out several tiny butterflies using the butterfly cutter/veiner. Dust some of the butterflies with myrtle satin dust, and the others with bridal satin and plum petal dust. Allow the butterflies to dry a little in natural wing positions before attaching to the cake using royal icing, softened sugarpaste or even clear alcohol.

Assembly

5 Tape together three orchid stems using the buds, flowers, aerial roots and foliage onto 18-gauge wire. You will also need a few leaf stems to add to the display.

6 Insert two posy picks into the large cake, just behind the top tier. Fill the picks with almond paste and then position the flower and leaf stems into them. The spray at the front of the cake is tricky to attach. Insert the pick into the side of the cake, and fill with almond paste. Position the flower stem in front of the pick and, using a piece of covered 20-gauge wire, form a staple long enough to hold the flowers in place, and fit into the posy pick. Re-arrange the position of the flowers, buds and foliage to create an attractive display.

Papilionanthe orchid

A genus of ten species native to the Asian tropics, *Papilionanthe*, or the butterfly orchid, was classified as a *Vanda* orchid; today they are known as 'terete vandas' because of their leaves, unlike the flat leaves of true vandas. They produce showy flowers in white, pink and magenta. The hybrid 'Miss Joaquim' is the national flower of Singapore.

Materials

White and pale holly/ivy flowerpaste

18-, 22-, 24-, 26- and 28-gauge white wires

Vine green, primrose, lemon, edelweiss African violet, foliage green and forest green petal dusts

Deep magenta craft dust

White and nile green floristry tape

Quarter glaze (optional)

Isopropyl alcohol

Equipment

Papilionanthe cutters (TT 813–816) or templates (p 154)

Amaryllis veiner (optional)

Silk veining tool (HP)

Very large rose petal veiner (GI)

Plain edge cutting wheel (PME)

Column

1 Roll a piece of white flowerpaste into a ball and then into a teardrop shape. Measure the length of the column against the throat petal (labellum) – it should be no longer than the section from the pointed base of the cutter to the start of the two side sections of the petal.

2 Hollow out the underside of the column using the rounded end of a celstick or ceramic tool. Press the length of the column against the length of the tool to create a natural shape to the column. As you are doing this, pinch a very subtle ridge to the back of the column.

3 Attach a tiny ball of paste onto the column, partially tucked under the hollow and partially on show. Indent the ball with a sharp scalpel to create two sections = the anther cap.

sometimes easier to do this when the column is completely dry.

Labellum (lip/throat)

5 Roll out some white flowerpaste leaving a thick ridge down the centre; this gives the petal a little extra support. Cut out the throat petal shape using either the cutter or a sharp scalpel and the template on page 154. Vein the petal using either the amaryllis veiner or the ceramic

shape. Pinch two small ridges at the base of the petal using a pair of angled tweezers – optional as you can barely see them in the finished flower.

7 Place the petal onto a pad and hollow out the two side sections using a small metal ball tool or celstick. Next, moisten the 'V' shape at the sides of the base of the petal. Place the dried column (hollow side down) against the petal. Carefully pull

4 Bend an open loop in the end of a 22-gauge white wire. Hold the hook with pliers and bend to form a ski stick shape. Moisten the hook and pull through the column about a third of the way from the anther cap. Embed the hook into the paste, then pinch the column from behind to secure it in place. To hide the hook, you will need to add a ball of paste over the top and blend it into the main body of the column—it is

silk veining tool to create fan formation veins.

6 Frill the two front sections of the petal using the silk veining tool – I usually rest the petal over my index finger to frill the petal. The two front sections are usually quite frilly. The two side sections need to be frilled only slightly. Pinch the length of the petal down the centre to create a subtle ridge and angle to the lip

the two side sections up onto the column. These side sections should meet over the column and in some cases overlap very slightly. Curl back the edges of the two side sections slightly. Allow to dry a little before colouring.

Colouring

8 Dust the base of the throat with a very light dusting of vine green. Mix together primrose and lemon petal dusts and add some colour to the inside of the throat, bringing a little yellow down onto the main section of the lip. Mix together some deep magenta craft dust with edelweiss petal dust, then dust around the edges of the throat petal. Next, add depth by using only deep magenta craft dust with a touch of African violet petal dust added – this colour needs to be kept at the centre of the petal and should form a border around the yellow on the throat. Add

Lateral petals

9 Roll out some white paste thinly, leaving a thick ridge at the centre for the wire. Cut out a wing petal shape using either the cutter or template and sharp scalpel. Insert a moistened 28-gauge white wire into the base of the petal, holding the paste firmly between your finger and thumb to prevent the wire piercing through the petal. Pinch the paste to secure it to the wire. Soften the edges of the petal using a ball tool or celstick.

attached back to front and then twisted forwards as a correction! It is sometimes easiest to tape the wing petals in place while they are still slightly soft and then reshape them.

Dorsal and lateral sepals

11 Roll out and cut out the three lateral sepal shapes as for the wing petals. Insert a 28-gauge wire into each petal. Soften the edges and vein using the rose petal veiner. Pinch each petal to accentuate the central vein.

some fine painted lines to the lip by diluting some of the deep magenta craft dust/African violet petal dust mix with clear alcohol. Use a fine paintbrush to create a series of fine veins that should fan out over the labellum. Try to add a few lines to the two cupped side sections too. There are, however, some orchid varieties that have quite plain lips, while others have tiny spots of colour distributed over the surface.

10 Place the petal into the large rose petal veiner and press firmly to create strong veining. Softly frill the edges of the petal using the silk veining tool (very gently). Again, it is best to do this against your index finger as it creates a much softer finish. Pinch the petal from the base to the tip. Repeat to make two wing petals. There is a curious twist at the base of these two petals – it looks almost as if the petals have been

Allow to firm up slightly over a gentle curve before taping behind the wing petals. As the petals are still soft, you should be able to reshape them to form a more natural shaped flower.

Colouring

12 Dust all of the outer petals with a light mixture of deep magenta craft dust, edelweiss and African violet petal dusts. The two wing petals will need a little more colour, but it should fade out gradually towards the petal edges.

Ovary

13. Wrap a sausage of pale green paste around the stem to form the ovary; work the paste between your fingers and thumb to thin it down the back. Create a series of lines down the back using the plain edge cutting wheel. Curve the stem gently. Dust the ovary and the back of the flower with vine green. Darken the ovary

slightly at the base with foliage green petal dust.

Buds

14. The buds to this orchid are a very odd shape – they look a bit like abstract teddy-bear heads! Roll a ball of white paste. Insert a hooked moistened 26- or 24-gauge wire into the base of the bud. First of all, pinch two pointed 'ears' on the top of the bud. Next, pinch a pointed nose at

the base. Then pinch a ridge on either side. Divide the surface of the bud using a scalpel to create two curved petal shapes over the front of the bud. Repeat to make buds in various sizes. Add a much finer ovary to the back of each bud. Dust with vine green and a little of the flower colour. The smaller buds will be more green than pink.

15. Tape the buds alternately onto an 18-gauge wire using half width

tape. Add the flowers. Dust the stems with foliage, forest and edelweiss.

Aerial roots

16. Tape over a short length of 26-gauge wire with half width tape. Leave a little of the newly taped length and then tape down again. Repeat this again leaving a little more length this time – to create an aerial root that is thinner at the tip than at the base. Bend to give a root shape.

Leaves

17. Insert a 26-gauge wire into a ball of green flowerpaste. Quickly work the paste down the wire to create the length of the leaf. Smooth the leaf between your palms. Trim off any excess. Create a fine central vein using the plain edge cutting wheel. Bend the leaf slightly to give a natural appearance. Make lots of leaves in varying sizes. Dust with forest, foliage and edelweiss petal dusts.

18. Starting with a small leaf, tape the leaves onto an 18-gauge wire with half width green tape. Occasionally add an aerial root with a leaf. Continue adding leaves along the required length. Dust the main stem as the leaves. Catch the base and tips of the aerial roots with vine green petal dust.

Slipper Orchid Plant

Creating a pot plant can be a fun and interesting task for the sugar flower maker. Here, the slipper (*Paphiopedilum*) orchid has been displayed at its best, with a long slender stem allowing the unusual shaped flowers to hang gracefully above the strong structured foliage of the plant. The plant has been displayed in a real plant pot with orchid bark chips and moss to cover the medium in which it has been arranged. A cake could be made to look like a plant pot and used in the same way with pieces of sugar bark (page 64) to hide the mechanics. *Tony*

Slipper orchid

There are over 60 species of *Paphiopedilum*, commonly known as slipper orchids, that extend from China to the Himalayas into India, Southeast Asia to New Guinea. Slipper orchids have been hybridized from the early days of orchid breeding, with plants in collections over 150 years old. This is the hybrid *Paphiopedilum helvetia*.

Materials

Pale melon, white, pale yellow, pale green and mid holly/ivy flowerpaste
18-, 20-, 22-, 24- and 26-gauge white wires
Primrose, plum, thrift, vine green, holly/ivy, moss green and forest green petal dusts
Full and half glaze
Nile green floristry tape

Equipment

Slipper orchid cutter set (TT881–884) or templates (p 153)
Card or thin plastic
Plain edge cutting wheel (PME)
Slipper orchid veiner set (GI)

Slipper (labellum)

1 The slipper is the most difficult part of this flower – it requires time both to make and to dry. Trace out the slipper template onto a piece of card or thin plastic. Roll out well kneaded pale melon flowerpaste (not too thinly), leaving the paste slightly thicker at the centre. Place the slipper template on the paste and cut out the shape. If you have the cutters, use the labellum cutter for this.

2 Put the slipper shape on a pad and soften the edges, especially the upper edges, with the rounded end of a large celstick. Hollow out the base on either side of the thick ridge with either the celstick or a large ball tool. Moisten one side of the bottom curved edge of the slipper. Use egg white for this only.

3 You will need to overlap the two bottom curved edges of the

carefully curl the top cut edges in towards each other. Use the plain edge cutting wheel to add a central vein to the front of the slipper orchid. Bend a hook in the end of a 20-gauge wire. Cover the wire with some white flowerpaste that has been softened and mixed with fresh egg white. Pull the hooked wire through the centre and at an angle. Then squeeze the various parts together slightly so that they merge completely. Allow to dry.

of the slipper around the rounded tip of the labellum. Allow to dry before dipping into a full glaze. Pour out the excess glaze from the slipper and repeat until you have the desired finish. Leave aside to dry.

Column
6 Roll a ball of well kneaded pale yellow paste into a cone shape. Flatten out the base of the cone and pinch one part into a point.

flowerpaste. Use the rounded end of a large celstick to help achieve the shape of the slipper throat, and press the join in the petal firmly with your thumb. Bend the join further by pressing the rounded end of the celstick against it.

4 Place the slipper on the pad and continue to cup and hollow out the shape using the rounded end of the celstick. At the top of the slipper,

Colouring
5 Dust the slipper lightly with primrose dusting powder. Add depth to the base of the slipper by applying a light dusting of plum and thrift mixture, making the colour slightly heavier at the rounded end of the labellum. Dust the edge of the lip with the plum/thrift mixture. Dilute some of the plum/thrift mixture with a little water. Use this mixture to paint some fine veins onto the surface

7 Next, use a sharp scalpel to mark out a central vein. Try to pull the side that is opposite the point into a 'V'-shape (the finished column should resemble that of a heart). Insert some softened flowerpaste into the dried slipper and attach the column. Dust with vine and primrose. Using a cocktail stick or a scriber, add a dent into the centre of the column. Add a few spots of diluted thrift into the actual labellum.

Lateral petals

8 Roll out some pale melon flowerpaste, leaving a thick ridge at the centre for a wire. Use either the flat side of one of the double-sided petal veiners (or a template page 153) with a sharp scalpel or a cutter to cut out the petal shape. Insert a moistened 26-gauge wire into the thick ridge of the flowerpaste and pinch the base of the petal to secure it. Position the flowerpaste on a pad

Dorsal sepal

9 Roll out pale melon flowerpaste. Then, using either the flat side of the dorsal veiner or the template from page 153, or a cutter, cut out the basic shape. Insert a 26-gauge white wire into the thick ridge and pinch the base into a sharp point. Soften the edges of the paste and then vein the surface using either the double-sided veiner or the dresden tool (the veins should curve out from the base

Colouring and assembly

11 First, dust the lateral sepals with pale primrose petal dust and then overdust at the wire end with some vine green petal dust. Dust the sepals from the tip, backwards with the plum/thrift mixture, making it darkest in the middle part of the sepals. Paint delicate spots onto the sepals. Paint a series of lines onto the base and dorsal petals – the dorsal petal should be slightly bolder. Add some

and soften the edges. Vein the surface using the double-sided petal veiner. (Alternatively, you can add freehand veins to the petals with the fine end of a dresden tool.) Turn the petal over and mark a strong central vein - this should form a ridge on the reverse side of the petal. Allow the flowerpaste to firm slightly before twisting the petal into an attractive spiral. Repeat this process to make two wing petals.

and back again at the tip). Curl back the edges at the base of the sepal. Leave the paste aside to firm up a little, before colouring.

Base sepal

10 Repeat the process described in step 9 to make the base sepal. Use either the base sepal template or the double-sided veiner, or a cutter, to obtain the correct shape. Then leave the paste to dry completely.

delicate spots to the back of each of the sepals.

12 The wing petals should have some tiny pimples left by the veiner. Paint over each of the pimples with a small amount of colour and then add some fine veins to the bottom half of each petal.

13 Tape a couple of 18-gauge wires alongside the main stem using half width nile green floristry tape. Attach the wing petals to either side of the slipper and then add the dorsal and base sepals.

Ovary and bract

14 Attach a sausage of pale green flowerpaste to the back of the flower. Thin out either end of the sausage shape to make it look slightly padded at the centre. Use a pair of fine angled tweezers to create several

the ovary base. Dust the bract as for the ovary.

Leaves

16 Roll out some mid holly/ivy paste, not too thinly, leaving a thick ridge for the wire. Cut out the leaf freehand using the leaf template and a scalpel or cutting wheel.

17 Insert a moistened 24-, 22- or 20- gauge wire into the thick ridge.

green and forest green petal dusts. When dry, dip into a half glaze and dry again.

Bud

19 Roll a ball of paste into a blunt cone, insert a hooked 20-gauge wire into the centre and pinch firmly to attach. Before adding the bract, thicken the wire with both tape and paste. Add the bract as described in step 15. Colour the buds quite dark

long ridges over the surface of the ovary, from the top to the bottom. Next, gently curve the stem. The ovary and the stem should then be dusted with holly/ivy and vine green powders. Add a touch of thrift to the back of the flower.

15 Roll out pale green flowerpaste and cut out the bract shape using the template or the cutter. Soften and vein the bract shape and attach it to

Position the paste on a pad and soften the edges. Vein the centre of the leaf strongly using the fine end of the dresden tool. Turn the shape over against the pad and hollow out the underside. Pinch the leaf between your finger and thumb. Repeat to make leaves of several sizes.

Colouring

18 Dust the leaves first with holly/ivy, then overdust with moss

with thrift and a little holly/ivy at the base. When dry, dip in half glaze.

Assembly

20 Tape the flowers and buds to a strengthened stem. Insert into the staysoft and secure. Add a bract half way between the lower flower and the surface of the pot, colouring it as described for the flower. Add wired leaves around the stem to make a growing plant. Adjust the leaves.

Oriental Delight

A delightful and dramatic spray of oriental bamboo orchids and lace-cap hydrangea adorn this beautiful single tier cake that would be suitable for a birthday, anniversary or small wedding reception. The flowers have been complemented with a delicate brush embroidered leaf and swirl side design. *Alan*

Cake and decoration

25cm (10in) curved leaf cake
35cm (14in) curved leaf cake board
1.25kg (2½lb) white almond paste
1.5kg (3¼lb) white sugarpaste
Royal icing
African violet, edelweiss and foliage green petal dusts
Broad magenta ribbon to trim board
Green paper-covered wire

Flowers

1 lace-cap hydrangea and foliage
3 bamboo orchids and foliage

Equipment

Nos. 1 and 2 piping tubes (tips)
Embroidery design templates (p 154)
Posy pick

Preparation

1 I brought a set of curved leaf tins from my last trip to Australia. Hopefully, these tins will soon be widely available. Alternatively, bake a teardrop shaped cake and carefully re-cut into a curved leaf shape. Brush the cake with apricot glaze and cover with almond paste. Allow to dry overnight. Moisten the surface with clear alcohol and then cover with white sugarpaste, using the curved edge smoother on the top surface of the cake, and the straight edge smoother on the sides.

2 Cover the cake board with white sugarpaste, then transfer the cake on top. Use the straight edge smoother to smooth the paste at the base of the cake to neaten the join. Allow to dry overnight.

3 Pipe a snail's trail around the base of the cake using some royal icing and a No. 2 piping tube (tip).

Side design

4 Trace the embroidery designs on page 154 onto either tracing paper or greaseproof paper, and then scribe them onto the cake. Pipe the main lines of the designs onto the cake using some white royal icing in a piping bag fitted with a No.1 piping tube. Outline the leaf shapes, and then carefully brush the outline from either edge of the piped leaf using a No.1 paintbrush (slightly moistened with water or clear alcohol). Try to keep the brush strokes smooth to the central vein to create an attractive leaf shape. Allow to dry.

5 Highlight the piped work using a small amount of African violet petal dust diluted with alcohol, and edelweiss petal dust. Paint in the leaves using foliage, edelweiss and clear alcohol.

Assembly

6 Attach a band of magenta ribbon to the board edge using a non-toxic glue stick. Tape the spray together using the hydrangea flower head as the starting point. Next, pull in the three orchid stems to create the focal point, and the basic outline of the spray. Add extra leaves to fill in any gaps. Finally, add two sets of curved green paper-covered wire to create a dramatic outline to the spray. Insert into the posy pick, then into the cake.

Lace-cap hydrangea

Although there are many cultivars of *Hydrangea macrophylla*, the species actually originated in China and Japan. What look like flowers on a hydrangea head are actually modified bracts – the true flowers are at the centre of the flower head and at the centre of each set of bracts. The flowers at the centre of the modified bracts are sterile. The fertile flowers are found *en masse* at the centre of the whole hydrangea flower head.

Materials
White and mid holly/ivy flowerpaste
18-, 22-, 24-, 26-, 28-, 30- and 33-gauge white wires
Fine white silk stamens
African violet, aubergine, forest green, foliage and vine green petal dusts
Deep magenta craft dust
White and nile green floristry tape
Half glaze

Equipment
Very small calyx cutter (CLC No.12) (optional)
Hydrangea petal cutters (TT) or templates (p 154)
Hydrangea bract cutters (TT 764, 765)
Large hydrangea petal veiner (GI)
Virginia creeper leaf cutters (SF) or p 154
Large, medium and small hydrangea leaf veiners (GI)
Plain edge cutting wheel or sharp scalpel
Stencil brush or new toothbrush (optional)

Buds
1 You will need to make buds for both the mass of florets at the centre of the hydrangea head and for some of the sterile 'flowers'. Cut several 33-gauge white wires into fifths and make a tiny hook in the end of each. (I usually use dry wires for this but you might prefer to moisten the hook to give extra hold.) Insert the hook into a tiny grain-shaped piece of white flowerpaste. Divide the surface of the

bud into five for the mass of florets, and into four for the large flowers. You can do this by using a sharp scalpel or plain edge cutting wheel, or by using a cage made from four or five 33-gauge wires (see p 10). You will need to make lots of these buds.

Flowers

2 There are both fertile and sterile flowers on a hydrangea head. The fluffy mass of flowers at the heart of the head are fertile, and can have four, five or six petals (even double flowers). The sterile flowers are

the stamens – in this instance with African violet petal dust and a touch of deep magenta craft dust. For pulled flowers, form a small cone shaped piece of white paste. Using fine scissors, cut into the rounded end to create four or five petals. Open up the petals and pinch the tip of each into a point between your finger and thumb. Flatten each petal, then rest the flower against your index finger and thin out the petals a little more using the broad end of a dresden tool. Open up the centre of the flower and thread the stamens

and fours. Roll out some white flowerpaste, leaving a thick ridge at the centre (a grooved board could be used if preferred). Cut out a bract shape (usually two small, two large – but occasionally all the same size). Insert a moistened 30-gauge white wire into the thick ridge of the petal – about quarter to half way.

4 Place the bract onto a pad and soften the edges of the paste, working half on the paste and half on the pad, with a metal ball tool – do not frill.

found at the centre of the modified bracts, often looking at first glance like a stamen at the centre of a flower. The flowers can be made as pulled flowers or with a tiny daphne cutter (four petals), or tiny calyx cutter (five petals). I prefer to pull these tiny flowers – whichever method you decide, you will first need to glue five short stamens onto the end of a short length of 33-gauge wire. Allow to dry. Dust the tips of

through the centre. Neaten the back of the flower and remove any excess paste. Make lots of flowers. Dust each with African violet (or your chosen colour).

Modified bracts (petals)

3 You might first think that these are the petals of the hydrangea; they are, in fact, coloured modified bracts. These can be in threes, fours, fives or more – I usually make them in threes

5 Vein using the double-sided hydrangea petal (bract) veiner. Pinch the base and the tip of the petal to emphasize the central vein. Allow to rest on dimpled foam. Repeat to make the required number. Another variety of hydrangea has jagged edged bracts – if you want to create this effect, use the broad end of the dresden tool to pull out the edges of the bract. Soften the bract as described in step 4 and then vein.

Colouring and assembly

6 Dust the base of each bract with African violet petal dust, tapering the colour into the central vein.

7 Tape four bracts around a single bud or sterile four-petalled pulled flower using half width white floristry tape. Usually the two smaller bract shapes are opposite each other with the two larger ones positioned in between and slightly behind them.

Tape the fertile flowers and buds into small groups using white tape.

Leaves

8 Roll out mid green paste, leaving a thick ridge. Cut out the leaf shape, using Virginia creeper cutters or the leaf templates on page 154. Or, cut out a basic leaf shape and freehand serrations from the leaf edge using scissors. Insert a moistened 26-, 24- or 22-gauge wire into the thick ridge.

9 Soften the edges of the leaf using a metal ball tool, working half on the paste and half on the pad. Vein the leaf using the appropriate sized hydrangea leaf veiners. Pinch the leaf from the base to the tip to create a strong central vein. Allow the leaf to firm up before dusting.

10 Dust the edges of each leaf with aubergine petal dust. Dust the leaf from the base with forest green,

fading out to the edges. Overdust with foliage green and finally vine green petal dust. The backs of the leaves should be much paler so use only a little colour here. Dry further before dipping into a half glaze.

Assembly

11 Tape a small cluster of fertile flowers and buds onto the back of some of the bract flowers. Tape several clusters onto the end of an

18-gauge wire using half or even full width nile green floristry tape. Next, add the bracts (with buds and flowers) around the stem – you should aim to keep the small clusters of flowers quite flat and receded slightly. Thicken the stem with more full width tape or a layer of shredded kitchen paper taped over with nile green tape. Add the leaves onto the stem as opposite pairs, starting with the smaller leaves and working

gradually up to the larger ones. Dust the main stem with foliage green, and perhaps a touch of aubergine too. Seal the colour onto the stem by rubbing a thin layer of hi-tack glue over it.

12 For a speckled effect flower head, simply dilute some colour with isopropyl alcohol and use a stencil brush to flick the colour onto the flower head.

Bamboo orchid

I have made one of the smaller bamboo orchids *(Arundina graminifolia)* – in the wild they range in size from 4cm (2½in) to 8cm (3in) wide! Its name refers to the very long reed-like stems and slender bamboo-like leaves of the plant. Growing widely across Asia, there are about eight species of *Arundina* orchids; they can be white, flesh coloured, pink or magenta.

Materials
White and mid green flowerpaste
18-, 22-, 24-, 26- and 28-gauge white wires
Lemon, African violet, edelweiss, vine green, foliage green and forest green petal dusts
Deep magenta craft dust
White floristry tape
Half glaze

Equipment
Bamboo orchid cutters
(TT 817–820) or templates (p 154)
Silk veining tool (HP)
Very large rose petal veiner (GI)
Angled tweezers
Tulip leaf veiner (GI)
Plain edge cutting wheel (PME)

Column
1 Roll a small ball of white flower-paste, then form it into a very narrow teardrop shape. Moisten the end of a 22-gauge white wire and insert it into the narrow end of the teardrop, so that it is inserted into about two-thirds of the length of the column. Hollow out the length of the under-side of the column by pressing the wired column against the rounded end of the ceramic silk veining tool or

celstick. Try to pinch a subtle ridge to create the 'backbone' of the column. Thin the very sides of the column at the top by simply pressing the edges against the sides of the veining tool. Add a tiny ball of paste at the top of the column to represent the anther cap. Indent the centre of the anther cap using a sharp scalpel. Dry.

Labellum (lip/throat)

2 Roll out white paste, leaving the central area slightly thicker. Cut out the petal, using either the throat petal cutter or the template. Vein the surface of the petal using the veining tool in a fan formation – try not to broaden the petal shape too much.

3 Using the silk veining tool again, increase the pressure on the edges of the petal to give a very frilled edge. Add extra frilling using a cocktail or metal frilling stick if necessary.

4 Using angled tweezers, pinch two long ridges, close to one another, down the centre of the petal (this is why the paste needs to be left thicker at the centre). Place the petal onto a pad, and cup the two side sections slightly. Moisten the base and the sides of the petal slightly with fresh egg white, and then wrap the petal around the wired column. Curl back the edges of the petal. Allow to firm up a little before colouring the lip.

Colouring

5 Dust the two ridges at the centre of the throat with lemon petal dust. The colour of the lip will depend upon the exact variety you are making; I have used deep magenta craft dust and African violet. The upper surface of the throat should be strongly coloured, but only the edges on the back should have colour on them – the main part of the back should be white or paler pink.

Lateral petals

6 Roll out some white flowerpaste thinly using a large celstick, leaving the thick ridge at the centre for the wire. Cut out the wing petal shape.

7 Insert a short length of moistened 28-gauge white wire into the thick ridge of the petal. Soften the edge of the petal gently using a medium ball tool – do not try to frill the paste at this stage. Vein the petal using the double-sided rose petal veiner – you need to use the back of the veiner to create a ridge on the front surface of the orchid petal.

8 Some varieties have slightly frilled wing petals and others have very straight edges. Softly frill the edges using the silk veining tool. Pinch the petal at the base and the tip. Allow to firm up over a gentle curve. Repeat to make two wing petals.

Dorsal and lateral sepals

9 Roll out white paste, creating a thick ridge at the centre again. Cut out a sepal shape. Insert a moistened 28-gauge white wire into about half the length of the sepal. Soften the edges, and then vein using the rose petal veiner – the central ridge will be on the back. Pinch the sepal to a sharp point at the tip, and gently at the base. Make three sepals. Firm up a little before colouring.

you to reshape the final flower. Tape the wing petals onto either side of the throat using half width white tape. Next add the three outer sepals – the legs should be tucked very close to the underside of the orchid throat. Dust the tips, back of the flower and the stem with vine green.

Buds

12 Bend an open hook in the end of a 24-gauge wire. Roll a ball of

floristry tape. Dust the bud as for the outer petals of the orchid. Add a touch of vine and foliage green.

Leaves

14 Roll out a long length of mid green paste either using a grooved board or by rolling and leaving a thick ridge at the centre. Cut out a long narrow leaf shape. Insert a 26-, 24- or 22-gauge moistened wire into about half the length of the leaf.

Colouring and assembly

10 Colour each of the petals and sepals with a very light dusting of deep magenta craft dust, African violet and edelweiss petal dusts mixed together. Add most of the colour at the base, tapering down the centre of each petal/sepal. The wing petals should have more colour.

11 Assemble the orchid before the petals are completely dry, allowing

paste and then form it into a chubby cone shape. Moisten the hook and insert it into the base of the cone. Pinch the base of the bud to secure it neatly to the wire. Divide the bud into the three. Create a series of fine veins over the surface using a sharp scalpel. Pinch the tip of the bud into a sharp curved point.

13 Tape over the stem with a couple of layers of half width white

15 Place the leaf on a pad and soften the edges – do not frill. Vein the leaf using the double-sided tulip leaf veiner, or on a piece of dried sweet corn or even crepe paper. Pinch the leaf to emphasize the central vein from the base to the tip. Allow to firm up a little before colouring. Make in various sizes. Dust each leaf with forest green and foliage petal dusts. Dip each leaf in turn into a jar of half glaze.

Autumn Sunset

A vibrantly coloured heart shaped cake that would be wonderful for an autumnal celebration. *Laeliocattleya* orchids, *Oncidium* orchids, spiky leucadendron, weeping fig leaves and autumn berries have been spectacularly combined in vivid colours to create a very modern design. *Tony*

Cake and decoration

20cm (8in) heart shaped cake
800g (1¾lb) white almond paste
1kg (2¼lb) white sugarpaste
28cm (11in) heart cake board
3mm peach and mulberry purple ribbon
9mm feathered edge peach ribbon
Flowerpaste
Honiton lace cutter (DL)
Violet, apricot and tangerine petal dusts
3 laeliocattleya 'Barbara Bell' apricot(p 58)
4 leucadendron stems
5 stems of viburnum berries (see step 4)
13 camellia leaves or similar foliage
9 red oncidium orchids
5 stems of weeping fig (p 79)
Posy pick

Preparation

1 Brush the cake with apricot glaze and cover with almond paste. Leave to dry. Moisten with clear alcohol and cover the cake and board with sugarpaste.

2 Attach a thin band of mulberry ribbon to the cake base and thin band of peach ribbon above, overlapping slightly. Secure a band of mulberry ribbon to the bottom edge of the board, then add the peach ribbon just above, with the mulberry showing.

3 Stiffen the flowerpaste with cornflour. Place a little white fat at the corner of the board. Roll out the flowerpaste thinly and remove the cut lace from the cutter by pressing into the fat. This will cause suction, which will enable the cut lace pieces to be removed from the cutter. Measure the circumference of the cake and calculate the number of lace pieces you need. Place them on a flat, preferably porous, surface to dry. Dust the tips of the lace using violet and apricot dusts. Attach the lace to the cake with royal icing.

4 Make the laeliocattleya orchid as page 58, using paprika flowerpaste.

Dust the petals with apricot petal dust, the throat with apricot and throat edge with tangerine dust.

5 For the viburnum berries, roll pale green paste into small balls and insert a moistened hooked 30-gauge white wire through each berry. Add a small black stamen into the ends. Colour the berries with vine and pale moss green, the sides with skintone and the stems with pale green. Tape the berries into clusters, dip in half glaze, then tape onto a 20-gauge wire.

Assembly

6 First tape the three laeliocattleya orchids to a sprig of leucadendron. Add the green berries to the top of the orchids, filling in the gaps. Add a few of the camellia leaves, then the remaining leucadendron sprigs in-between each of the orchids.

7 Finally, thread the red oncidium orchids into the spray at random, filling any gaps. Add the camellia leaves or other foliage to the base and then the weeping fig leaves.

8 Place the stem of the spray into the posy pick and insert into the centre of the cake.

Oncidium orchid

There are more than 400 known species of *Oncidium* orchids with a wide range of habit, colour and inflorescence style. The flower illustrated here is *Oncidium ornithorrhynchum* from Mexico and Guatemala. The plant flowers during the autumn and early winter, producing highly scented pretty rose-pink flowers.

Materials

26-, 28- and 30-gauge white wire

White and claret flowerpaste

African violet, yellow and moss green petal dusts

Deep magenta craft dust

Nile green floristry tape

Equipment

Oncidium orchid veiners

Oncidium orchid cutters (TT 856–859) or templates (p 155)

Column

1 To use the column veiner, place a small cone of white paste on a 26-gauge wire and put into the column veiner, Remove the paste and flute the sides with a dresden tool.

2 Alternatively, roll a very small piece of white paste onto a 26-gauge white wire, hollowing out the under side and fluting either side of the column with a dresden tool and forming a very small anther cap on the tip of the column.

Labellum (lip/throat)

3 Roll out a small piece of claret flowerpaste, leaving a small ridge in the centre of the paste, Using the oncidium orchid cutter or the template provided on page 155, cut out a lip with a sharp scalpel. Insert a moisten 28-gauge wire into the ridge.

4 Roll a very small ball of claret flowerpaste and press it into the dip in the top half of the veiner to form the raised platform, Soften the edges of the lip petal and place in the veiner.

5 Remove from the veiner, place on a board and gently flute the edge of the lip with the dresden tool. Very carefully pinch the centre vein to a point. Place on dimpled foam to dry.

7 Roll and cut out one dorsal sepal petal and two side petals using the small straight petal cutters or templates. Moisten a 28-gauge wire and insert into the thicker end of the petals. Soften the edges and vein using the veiner. Very lightly flute the sides with a dresden tool.

Colouring
8 Dust the column by mixing a little African violet petal dust with deep

yellow petal dust with some clear alcohol.

11 Dust the sepals and petals with deep magenta craft dust.

Assembly
12 Tape the column to the lip using nile green floristry tape.

13 Add the two lateral petals – these are the legs to the orchid. Tape

Sepals and petals
6 Roll out claret flowerpaste, leaving a ridge in the centre of the paste. (You will only need a small amount of flowerpaste.) Cut out two lateral petals using the curved petal cutters or templates. Moisten a 28-gauge wire and insert into the thicker end of the petals. Soften the edges and vein using the appropriate veiner, then very lightly flute the sides with a dresden tool.

magenta craft dust, then dust the top of the column and the inside of the column, leaving the original sides of the flowerpaste white.

9 Dust the lip with African violet petal dust and deep magenta craft dust, drawing the brush up the petal to the raised platform.

10 Paint the top side of the raised platform by mixing together a little

them close together and tuck them underneath the lip. Add two arm petals and centre dorsal sepals.

Buds
14 Roll a very small ball of pale claret paste onto a hooked 26-gauge wire, tapering the paste to a point.

15 Dust the larger buds with deep magenta craft dust and the smaller buds with moss green petal dust.

Leucadendron

This leucadendron has been copied from a dried stem. For a fresh stem the instructions are the same, but the colouring will vary. Part of the *Proteaceae* family from South Africa, they have male and female flowers on separate plants. The former has fluffy flowers and the female ones (described here) resemble small cones; both have colourful modified bracts. Leucadendrons are very popular with florists.

Materials

White, pale autumn gold and pale green flowerpaste
20-, 28- and 30- gauge white wires
Nutkin brown, white, autumn gold, moss green and holly/ivy petal dusts
Olive green floristry tape

Equipment

Mould for centre (made from silicone plastique, see p 8)
Leucadendron sepal and leaf cutters (TT 873–877) or templates (p 155)
Solomon's seal leaf veiner (GI)

Preparation

1 It is best to make a mould of the cone-like flower centre of a real leucadendron using silicone plastique. First, you will need a dry stem of leucadendron – this may be obtained from your local florist.

2 Mix a small amount of silicone plastique, making a number of pea-size balls. Press these well into the sides and top of stem head. To thicken and

strengthen the mould, mix another small amount of silicone plastique, rolling a strip long enough to wrap around and cover the stem head.

3 When the silicone plastique has set (this takes approximately 20 minutes), with great care, cut down one side of the mould and across the bottom. Carefully open out the mould in order to remove dried flower head.

burn. This will caramelize the sugar and set very quickly, giving you an almost instant bond.

6 Put the mould into a freezer for about half an hour to harden. When ready, gently ease open the mould and remove the sugar stem head. Allow this to dry completely, after which any excess paste can be removed from the sides of the head to neaten.

Insert a moistened 30-gauge wire into the ridged end and soften the edges, then vein the bracts with the Solomon's seal veiner. Remove from the veiner and pinch the tips to form a sharp point. Leave to dry. Dust all the bracts with autumn gold, adding a little moss green to shade the two larger size bracts.

Larger bracts
9 Repeat the above using pale green

Female flower cone
4 Roll two equal balls of white flowerpaste and press them into either side of the mould, bringing the two sides together.

5 Heat a hooked 20-gauge wire over a naked flame (a cigarette lighter or night light is the best option) and push into the flowerpaste in the mould. Be careful not to push it in too far as it may cause the mould to

Colouring
7 Dust the flower head heavily with nutkin brown petal dust. Overdust with white petal dust to give a frosted cobweb effect.

Small modified bracts
8 Roll out some pale autumn gold flowerpaste, leaving a small ridge at one end. Using the three smaller size bract cutters or the templates on page 155, cut out three of each.

paste and the two larger bract cutters in the set to cut out three of each size. Soften and vein as before. Dust with holly/ivy mixed with white.

Assembly
10 Tape the bracts around the flower cone centre using half width olive tape. Start with the smallest bracts and gradually increase them in size, working around and down the stem. Steam to set the colour.

Glowing Embers

The flower which inspired this Christmas cake was the striking orange orchid, guaranteed to brighten a winter's day. The colours of the Christmas bells and cherries echo those of the orchid, with their names providing a further link with this season. *Tombi*

Cake and decoration

20cm (8in) round fruit cake
850g (1lb 14oz) white almond paste
1kg (2¼lb) white sugarpaste
28cm (11in) round cake board
Wide gold ribbon to trim cake
White ribbon to trim board

Flowers

3 bunches of Christmas cherries
3 brassavolalaeliocattleya orchids
3 stems of Christmas bells

Equipment

Large posy pick

Preparation

1 Fill any dents and holes in the cake with almond paste. Roll out the almond paste, smoothing it with the smoother before applying it to the cake. Brush the cake with warm apricot glaze, lift the almond paste by draping it over the rolling pin and gently lower it onto the cake, smoothing with your hand to ensure no air bubbles are trapped. Smooth the almond paste onto the cake and cut off any excess. Ensure the coating is really smooth by using a pair of smoothers.

2 Give the almond paste a final polish with a piece of polished almond paste, being very careful not to stop or the almond paste will stick together. Set the cake aside in a cake box to dry.

3 On the same day that you marzipan the cake, cover the board with sugarpaste, cutting out a circle from the centre of the board using the tin the cake was baked in as a guide. Set aside to dry.

4 Repeat the process of coating the cake, this time using Grand Marnier or Kirsch brushed onto the almond paste to help the sugarpaste stick to the cake. Trim off the excess paste, smooth and polish.

Assembly

5 Transfer the cake to the centre of the coated board. Fasten the wide gold ribbon around the base of the cake to disguise the join.

6 You can, if you wish, let down some sugarpaste with the Grand Marnier until it is of piping consistency and pipe a simple small snail's trail around the base of the cake. Trim the cake board with the white ribbon.

7 As the arrangement is close to the base of the cake, be very careful when inserting the large posy pick. It is best to cut the sugarpaste and remove some cake before inserting the pick so you don't crack the side of the cake. Always allow the pick to protrude slightly so it will be seen when the cake is cut.

8 First, tape the Christmas cherries and leaves into bunches.

9 Wire the orchids, Christmas bells and cherries into an attractive spray and insert into the posy pick. Make the final adjustments.

Brassavolalaeliocattleya

Although this orchid looks like a *Cattleya*, it is a trigeneric cross between *Brassavola*, *Laelia* and *Cattleya*, and named after Dora Louise Capen. It has elements of all three of these species. When I visited the Wyld Court Rain Forest, Newbury in Berkshire, on a cold, wet, overcast day, I saw this glorious flower glowing like burning embers in the dark of the rain forest and decided I must share this orchid in the book.

Materials

Pale yellow flowerpaste, using primrose and egg yellow petal dusts

18-, 24-, 26- and 28-gauge white wires

Scarlet craft dust

Primrose, egg yellow and vine green petal dusts

Nile green floristry tape

Equipment

Orchid cutters (TT 810–812) or templates (p 155)

Plain edge cutting wheel (PME)

Stargazer (B) veiner (GI)

Needle frilling tool (CC)

Silk veining tool (HP)

Column

1 Roll a small piece of pale yellow flowerpaste into a ball. Moisten the end of a third length 24-gauge wire and fasten the piece of paste onto the wire, working it into a small carrot shape. Place it firmly against the palm of your hand or a finger and roll a small metal ball tool from the wire towards the tip. This will both curve and cup the column. Gently pinch the tip to a rounded point.

2 Carefully mark two grooves towards the edge of the upper surface of the column. Take a tiny piece of paler yellow paste and roll it into a tiny ball. Moisten the underside of the tip of the column and attach the small ball of paste; then, using the cutting wheel, divide to form the pollinia. Set aside to dry.

Labellum (lip/throat)
3 Roll out a piece of pale yellow

then the needle frilling tool to frill the edge of the labellum very heavily on the five curves.

5 Moisten the centre back of the lip and extend along the smooth unfrilled lower edge. Fasten this onto the dried column. The two edges should be gently pinched together. Carefully turn back the petal above the column and gently pull down the lip. Set aside until leather hard.

Turn onto the palm of your hand with the underside of the petal uppermost. Use a dresden tool to ensure you have a raised centre on the upper side of the petal. While doing this, curve the petal slightly. With this orchid some of the petal tips curve back, but more flick forwards at the tip. Set aside until leather hard.

Sepals
8 Roll out a piece of pale yellow

paste, leaving a thickened ridge down the centre. Elongate the central part of the labellum. Dust the stargazer (B) veiner with a little cornflour and vein the labellum.

4 Use the needle frilling tool to mark a strong vein down the centre of the labellum. Carefully pinch two lines on either side of the wire at the base of the petal to create the pollen guides. Use the silk veining tool and

Lateral petals
6 Roll out a piece of flowerpaste with a thickened ridge down the centre (or on a grooved board). Insert a quarter length moistened 26-gauge wire into the ridge, taking it almost to the tip. Dust the veiner lightly and vein the petal.

7 Frill the edge of the petal heavily, first with the silk veining tool and then finishing with the frilling tool.

paste. Moisten a quarter length 26-gauge wire and place along the rolled-out piece of paste. Roll over the wire to imbed it in the paste. Fold back the paste to sandwich the wire and roll out again. Cut out the sepal with the long slender cutter, the wire extends from the slightly wider end. Vein the sepal in the veiner.

9 Use the dresden tool to emphasize the ridge on the sepals,

making sure the veins are raised on the upper surface of the sepal. Curve gently. Set aside until leather hard.

Colouring and assembly

10 It is essential to dust the scarlet colouring onto the petals before they are dry, being careful not to distort the shapes. Dust the colour most strongly onto the edges of the petal, lightening it on the lateral petals and sepals as you approach the centre.

of the lip; add the dorsal sepal behind and between the lateral petals, lastly adding the lateral sepals. Carefully tug each wire in turn to check fastening. Finish taping into a neat stem. Dust a little vine green dust behind the petals at the base and tapering up the centre back of the petals and sepals.

Bud

12 Take a medium sized piece of paste, roll into a barrel shape and

wires and gently mould the raised sections between your fingers to make an attractive bud – using a little artistic licence, you can curve them gently at the tip for a more elegant shape. Make several buds and leave to dry until leather hard.

14 Dust the scarlet colour most strongly onto the tip of the bud, taking it softly down the grooves. A little dust can then be dusted from

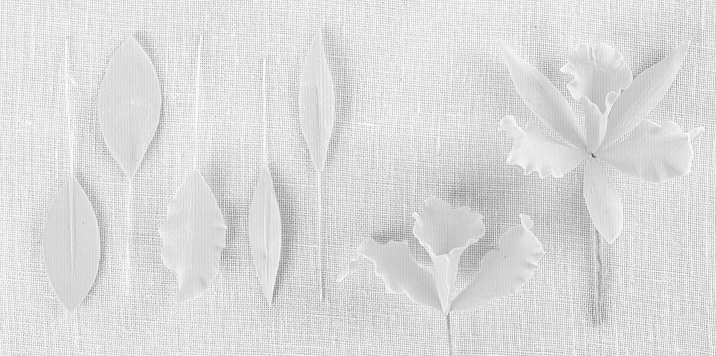

The yellow areas on some of the lips were left there quite deliberately: it is part of the coloration of this orchid. Dust a little primrose yellow onto the pollen guides and onto the base of the petals and sepals. I tend to do all this dusting once I have assembled the orchid, for a natural look.

11 To assemble the orchid, use half width tape to tape the lateral petals on either side and slightly to the back

insert a moistened third length of 18-gauge wire. Cut a 24-gauge wire into three equal lengths, tape one end together, bend a hook in the taped wire and tape over that. Separate into a cage in three equal divisions.

13 Put the wire end of the barrel shaped piece of paste into the cage, close the cage evenly, and pinch and pull very tightly so the wires cut into the paste. Carefully remove the cage

the tip of the bud down the raised sections of the bud. Finish by dusting a little vine green petal dust up the bud from the wire end, tapering the green colour so that it disappears into yellow before meeting the scarlet craft dust. Set the bud aside to dry completely.

15 When both the orchids and buds are completely dry, steam to set the colouring.

Christmas cherry

The Christmas cherry (*Solanum capsicastrum*) may be slightly pointed with the fruit ranging from greenish yellow through golden yellow, orange, scarlet and deep red to a rich aubergine, but there are some varieties where the fruit is very much the same shape and colour as cherry tomatoes.

Materials
Golden yellow and mid green flowerpaste
18-, 24-, 26-, 28-, 30- and 33-gauge white wires
Quarter and full glaze
Moss green, yellow, holly/ivy and African violet petal dusts
Scarlet craft dust
Mid green and twig floristry tape
Leaf cutters (TT 225–232) or templates (p 155)
Bittersweet leaf veiners to fit cutters (GI)

Fruit
1 Roll a ball of golden yellow paste (make the fruit in varying sizes); work it to a slight point so it is not quite round and make a small indentation at the tip. Leave to dry. When leather hard, dust the fruit; the smallest ones should be dusted with a little moss green; some should be left golden yellow, adding some scarlet craft dust to indicate the ripening fruit; liberally dust some fruit with the scarlet dust.

Set aside to dry before glazing with a full glaze for beautifully shiny fruit. Make leaves as the Radox Bouquet rose leaf on page 151. Dust with holly/ivy, moss, then African violet.

2 The plant grows in arching, brownish stems with clusters of leaves at the stem tip. The compound leaves are arranged alternately on either side of the stem, with the fruit growing from the leaf axils.

Christmas bells

These flowers are based on the Australian Christmas bell (*Blandfordia grandiflora*), which is one of the best known of the wild flowers of coastal eastern Australia. It generally flowers in rather swampy country shortly before Christmas, hence the common name. The bells vary from yellow to deep orange with a flame of red at the base, fading to the yellow or orange of the petals. I have used some artistic licence.

Materials

Pale yellow flowerpaste (coloured using egg yellow paste colour with a touch of primrose)

18- and 28-gauge white wires

Fine seedhead stamens

Non-toxic hi-tack glue

Scarlet craft dust

Twig floristry tape

Equipment

Cutters N4 and N5 (OP) or templates (p 155)

Silk veining tool (HP)

Buds

1 Roll a medium sized piece of pale yellow flowerpaste into a ball, moisten the end of a quarter length 28-gauge wire and insert it into the ball. Work the ball onto the wire, creating a sharp point at the end of the wire.

Work down the flowerpaste and create a slender, tapered neck behind the head of the bud. Using a six-wired cage, mark the bud. Remove any marks which may extend onto the neck of the bud. Create buds in several sizes. Set aside the buds until leather hard.

Flowers

2 Take four stamens and fold three in half, leaving the fourth much longer than the others. Cut off the excess cotton filaments. Dip the end of a quarter length 28-gauge wire into the glue and insert into the middle of the stamens. Hold tightly for a count of five. The stamens will be neatly stuck to the wire. Set the stamens aside to dry completely.

3 For the petals, roll a medium sized piece of flowerpaste into a ball, then roll into a cone, creating a slender

5 Open the throat of the flower with a large celstick to create the correct shape.

6 Insert a bunch of stamens into the throat of the flower, then work a slender neck just behind the bell of the flower, securing it to the wire. Set aside until leather hard.

Colouring

7 Dust the back of the flowers with

wires. The clusters can be in either odd or even numbers. The bud wires should be slightly shorter than the flower wires.

10 Carefully bend each stem into an attractive curve. Steam the flowers to set the colour.

Leaves

11 If you would like to use leaves with your arrangement, cut some

neck and back. Pinch the broad end into a circle and place on a board. Roll out the paste, not too fine. Cut out the petal shape.

4 Place the flower petals one by one onto a foam pad and work the back of each petal with the veining tool (try not to broaden the petals too much) – they need to curl backwards at the edge slightly and be textured.

scarlet craft dust, making the colour heaviest at the wire end. The top side of the petals should be left completely yellow/orange.

Assembly

8 Tape each bud and flower with half width twig floristry tape.

9 Tape the clusters of flowers and buds together into full length, three quarter and half length 18-gauge

strap shaped leaves with a cutting wheel, insert lengths of 20-gauge wires into them almost to the tip. Vein each leaf with a lily leaf veiner, then colour them with mid green petal dust. Bend each leaf into an attractive shape.

12 When completely dry, glaze the leaves with a half glaze. Tape a cluster of leaves at the base of the stems of the flowers.

Moth Orchid Plant

The glorious white varieties of the *Phalaenopsis* or moth orchid are particularly popular as wedding flowers, often being presented as long curving tied bouquets. In the container of this growing plant, either add cocoa bark from the garden centre or grate left-over brown flowerpaste. For clarity, I have shortened the flower spikes on this *Phalaenopsis* 'Aphrodite' but have kept the spike long on the *Phalaenopsis sanderiana* (page 70).   *Tombi*

Phalaenopsis 'Aphrodite'

Phalaenopsis, or moth orchids, flower up to three times a year bearing tall, long lasting flower spikes. They come in tones of white, yellow and pink, and may be spotted, striped, speckled or plain. The plants have three or four broad, curving leaves, with thick silvery white roots which frequently grow outside their pots.

Materials

White flowerpaste with small amount of yellow and mid green
18-, 20-, 22-, 24- and 26-gauge white wires (green may be used in the leaves)
Lemon yellow, vine green, holly/ivy, forest green and black petal dusts
Holly berry liquid colour
Deep magenta craft dust
Half glaze
Mother of pearl bridal satin dust
Nile green and twig floristry tape

Equipment

Phalaenopsis labellum cutter (J)
Templates (p 155)
Phalaenopsis orchid veiners (GI)
Needle frilling tool (CC)
Cymbidium orchid column mould (HH)
Plain edge cutting wheel (PME)

Dorsal and lateral sepals

7 Roll out white flowerpaste on a grooved board. Moisten a quarter length of 26-gauge wire and place it along the groove. Fold back the paste and roll out again. The length you choose to make these wires depends on your confidence. The shorter the wires are the less they will show through the sepals, but the sepals will break more easily without the wire to strengthen them.

2 Cut out the shapes, three for each orchid. Dust the veiner with cornflour and vein the shapes, one at a time. On some orchids, these sepals curve forwards, and on others they curve backwards. Shape according to your own preference.

3 Arrange the lateral sepals so that they oppose one another (left and right). Set the sepals on dimpled foam to dry.

Lateral petals
4 Roll out paste as before, inserting a moistened 26-gauge wire. Cut out the shapes and vein. If you wish, you can pinch a ridge on the upper surface of these petals. Place on dimpled foam to dry.

Labellum (lip/throat)
5 Use white paste and a 24-gauge wire for the labellum. Roll out the paste and position the wire as

described in step 1. For security, the wire can be taken to almost the tip of the labellum. Cut out the shape.

6 Place the labellum on a firm foam pad and work the edges of the shape. The two circular protrusions should be made slightly more oval. Work the centre of the labellum to get rid of the ridge created by the grooved board; then mark a vein down the centre of the labellum.

7 Using curved tweezers, mark the honey guides onto the lip on either side of the wire, between the two protrusions. Use a frilling tool to soften the edge of the protrusions and vein them gently.

8 Cut a piece of yellow paste, moisten the lip between the two protrusions (on top of the honey guides) and attach to the lip using the frilling tool. Use tweezers to shape it.

curve; on some flowers the tips can curve backwards slightly as it matures.

11 Roll a small piece of white flowerpaste into a fine thread. Place the labellum on the foam pad and place the thread of paste across the moistened tip of the labellum. Use a dresden tool to fasten the thread to the labellum. Carefully curve the labellum, curling the threads inwards towards the protrusions.

Tape the lateral petals immediately behind and alongside the labellum using nile green floristry tape, then tape in the dorsal sepal and lastly the lateral sepals.

13 Roll a small sausage of paste and place in the column mould. Use a metal ball tool to shape the piece of paste so it is hollow in the centre. Remove from the mould and pinch the tip to the typical point of the

9 Carefully dust the lip with lemon yellow; some of the dust is also brushed onto the underside of the labellum. Overdust with deep magenta craft dust until you achieve the colouring you want. Use a fine paintbrush and the holly berry liquid colour to paint spots and honey guide lines onto the labellum.

10 Carefully bend the two protrusions into a graceful inward

12 Arrange the piece so that the petals are allowed to dry in the appropriate curved shape. It is easier to put the flowers together when they are still leather hard rather than struggling with dry petals which will not bend. Bend the wire of the labellum at a right angle to the labellum. Using the fine brush and the holly berry liquid colour, paint small spots on the lateral sepals close to where the wire emerges from them.

moth's head. Cut off the column fairly short and moisten with egg white. Attach the column to the lip and to the front of the dorsal sepal. Use a dresden tool to ensure it is fastened firmly in place. Use softened paste to disguise any joins. Tape the stem of the flower – they are quite sturdy.

Buds

14 Make a hook in the end of a quarter length of 24-gauge wire. Roll a small piece of paste into a blunt cone. Moisten the end of the wire and insert into the upper edge of the cone. Shape into the typical bud shape with the stem emerging from near the top of the bud. Mark in the veins and the petal edges with the cutting wheel. Set aside to dry. Dust with vine green and holly/ivy. The smaller the bud the greener it is. If you prefer using artistic licence, you can keep some of the buds white.

template to cut out the leaf shape. Dust the veiner and mark the leaf. Remove from the veiner and shape the leaf. Place the leaf on dimpled foam to dry. When the leaves are leather hard, dust them with holly/ivy and forest green; dust until they are the colour you choose. If you wish, add a reddish edge to the leaves using deep magenta craft dust. Allow the leaves to dry completely before glazing with half glaze.

Assembly
18 Three-quarters fill a suitable container with staysoft. Tape the leaves together with full width tape. The leaves should be opposite and layered. Push the wire into the staysoft, allowing the leaves to be slightly proud. Insert the wires of the aerial roots into the staysoft below the leaves, curving over the edge of the container. Lastly, insert the stem of the flower spike as close to the

15 Tape the buds and flowers together into a graceful, curving spray. Steam to set the dust.

Leaves
16 Make a leaf veiner from the phalaenopsis using silicone plastique. Roll out mid green paste (fairly thick) and insert a moistened 18-gauge wire (half- to third-length depending on the size of the leaf) about two-thirds of the length of the leaf. Use a

Aerial roots
17 Roll a sausage of paste onto a 26-gauge wire right to the end. Work the paste onto the wire until you have a slightly tapering root. Place the root onto a foam pad and, using the veiner end of a dresden tool, shape the root. Curve it attractively. When leather hard, mix a little black dust into some holly/ivy green and lightly dust the root. Overdust with the bridal satin. Steam to set the dust.

centre of the leaves as you can get it. Dust the flower spike to look realistic.

Phalaenopsis sanderiana
19 Make this orchid and leaves as above. Make the veiners from silicone plastique. Cut out the lip and lateral petals from moth orchid cutters TT 28 and 30. Dust the flowers with lemon yellow, decorated with holly berry on the lip, and the petals, sepals and lip with deep magenta.

Pink Moth Orchid

Phalaenopsis, or moth orchids as they are more commonly known, are amongst the most popular exotic houseplants. They are also often used as wedding flowers for bouquets and arrangements as they survive so well as cut flowers. This stunning pink moth orchid (*Phalaenopsis sanderiana*) has been displayed in a ceramic container, showing the growing habit of the plant of long, gracefully arching flower spikes, its leathery foliage and curious thick silvery roots hanging over the edge of the pot. The flower is a smaller version of the white *Phalaenopsis* 'Aphrodite' described on page 64 and is created in a very similar way (see page 69).   *Tombi*

Golden Celebration

This stunning golden wedding anniversary cake was designed for my aunt and uncle. Lemon *Dendrobium* 'Montrose' orchids have been complemented beautifully with the addition of golden yellow roses, white bouvardia, birch, ivy and variegated hosta leaves.
Tony

Cake and decoration

15cm (6in) heart, 25cm (10in) round cake
1.5kg (3¼lb) white almond paste
1.75kg (4lb) white sugarpaste
20cm (8in) thin heart cake board
35cm (14in) round cake board
25mm ribbon to trim cake
5mm and 15mm ribbon to trim boards
4 open 'Golden Strike' roses (p 148)
6 'Golden Strike' rose buds
6 dendrobium 'Montrose' orchids
11 large ivy leaves
2 stems of bouvardia (p 117)
3 stems of birch leaves (p 135)
6 variegated hosta leaves
Posy picks
Small tilting perspex stand

Preparation

1 Brush the cakes with apricot glaze and cover with almond paste. Leave to dry. Moisten the surface with clear alcohol and cover with white sugarpaste using smoothers to achieve a good finish. Cover the boards with sugarpaste and position the cakes on top, making sure there is a neat join between the cake base and board.

2 Attach a band of ribbon to the base of each of the cakes using a tiny amount of royal icing. Secure a band of ribbon to the edge of each board using double-sided sticky tape.

3 For the 'Golden Strike' roses, follow instructions on page 148–151, then dust with lemon yellow mixed with a little egg yellow. Dust the backs of the petals with pale moss dust.

Assembly

4 Tape two of the dendrobium orchids onto three full length 20-gauge wires, then add two of the ivy leaves to the stems of each of the orchids to include the shorter ones.

5 Tape the two longer stems of orchids together, staggering them so there is a gap of approximately 4cm (1½in) between them. Add a rose bud, a single ivy leaf and a small stem of birch leaves. Make up the centre of the spray by taping three of the dendrobium orchids around the stem of bouvardia.

6 Add three open roses to the outer edge and a bud and the birch leaves to give the spray height. Add the long stem of orchids to the main spray, and then three hosta leaves.

7 For the small side spray, tape together three ivy leaves to a dendrobium orchid, then add a small rose bud and a small stem of birch leaves and one open rose. Add a stem of bouvardia and three hosta leaves.

8 Place the main spray into a posy pick and insert into the top of the cake, leaving it protruding slightly so it can be seen when the cake is cut. Either secure the smaller spray to the base of the larger cake by placing the spray into a small posy pick and inserting into the side of the cake, making sure it can be seen, or secure to the board with royal icing. Display the cakes using the tilted stand.

Dendrobium 'Montrose'

This attractive orchid is a hybrid form of *Dendrobium nobile*, without doubt one of the most popular and widely grown orchids in cultivation. In the wild, they can be found over a wide area of India, and as far south as Thailand and Vietnam. The species and hybrid forms of *Dendrobium nobile* are white, yellow, pink and purple, often with a very dark patch of colour in the throat of the flower.

Materials
Pale melon flowerpaste
24-, 26- and 28- gauge white wires
Ruby paste colour
Lemon, white, vine green and moss green petal dusts
Nile green floristry tape

Equipment
Dendrobium column mould (HH)
Dendrobium 'Montrose' cutters (TT 846–848) or templates (p 156)
Stargazer (B) veiner (GI)

Column
1 Place a small amount of paste into the column mould, pressing it well into the mould. Remove any excess from the mould. Using your thumb or a small piece of flowerpaste as a suction pad, remove the column from the mould, then hollow out the inside of the column with a small celstick.

2 Bend a small hook in a 24-gauge white wire, moisten and insert it through the hollow in the column and into the column head.

Labellum (lip/throat)
3 Roll out a piece of pale melon flowerpaste, leaving a small ridge in the centre. Cut out the labellum with the lip cutter. Place the lip on a board and flute around the edge with a dresden tool, then place the lip on a pad and soften the edge, pinching the tip to a point.

4 Using a pair of angled tweezers, pinch two ridges down the centre of the lip to form the platform. Moisten the base and attach to the column, then put aside to dry.

Lateral petals
5 Roll out a piece of pale melon flowerpaste, leaving a thicker ridge to the centre of one end. Using the lateral petal cutter, cut out one of each hand of the petals.

6 Insert a moistened 26-gauge white wire into the thicker ridge of the petals and place into the stargazer veiner to vein. Remove from the veiner, soften the edges and bend the petals to shape.

Colouring and assembly
7 Dilute a little ruby paste colour with clear alcohol and paint the markings on the lip. Mix lemon petal dust with a little white petal dust and

dust the edge of the lip. Dust the top of the orchid column with vine green petal dust.

8 Having the petal dust a little darker lemon in shade, petal dust the centre of the petals with a little on the edges.

9 Tape the two lateral petals to the back of the lip using the nile green floristry tape.

Sepals

10 Roll out a piece of flowerpaste with a ridge in the centre, making sure that it is large enough for the size of the cutter.

11 Cut out the sepals using the sepal cutter with the centre sepal over the ridge. Insert a 26-gauge wire into the ridge and vein each of the sepals separately. Soften the edges on a pad.

12 From the base of the stem, cut a ridge either side of the wire approximately 5mm (¼in) up the stem. This will allow the sepals to sit neatly to the back of the orchid.

13 While the sepals are still flexible, bend the wire at right angles and moisten either side of the ridge. Place on the back of the orchid, securing the wire to the stem with nile green

floristry tape and to the back of the orchid with edible glue. The sepals may need a little support with a piece of foam to dry.

14 Petal dust the back of the orchid with a mixture of vine and moss green petal dusts.

15 The leaves grow in a similar way to the curly dendrobium on page 16.

Hosta

Hostas, or plantain lilies, are natives of China and Japan. They have been cultivated in
Japan for many years. As a result, the true origin of many garden varieties is not
known. They are grown more for their handsome foliage than for their flowers,
although the flowers would be rather nice to make in sugar! They make an excellent
background leaf for many wedding sprays.

Materials
Mid green and pale melon flowerpaste

24-gauge white wire

Moss green and foliage green petal dusts

Half glaze

Nile green floristry tape

Equipment
Hosta leaf template (p 155)

Plain edge cutting wheel (PME)

1 Roll two balls of mid green and one
of pale melon paste into a long cigar
shape, then taper them off to a point
at both ends. Place the pale melon
paste in between the two pieces of
green paste. Roll out the paste
lengthways, leaving a ridge down the
centre of the paste and forming a
long strip of paste. Using the
template, carefully cut out the leaf.

2 Insert a moistened 24-gauge white
wire into the leaf ridge. Soften the
edges and use a dresden tool to make
the horizontal veins in the leaf. Pinch
a centre vein down the middle of the
leaf, and the tip to a sharp point,
gently curling the sides with a ball
tool. Dry on dimpled foam.

3 Lightly dust the leaves with moss
green to blend in the melon paste and
green, then petal dust the rest of the
leaf with a mixture of foliage green
and moss green. Steam the leaves,
then dip in half glaze.

Ivy

Ivies *(Hedera helix)* are very adaptable and decorative foliage plants which are used as both house and garden plants. Their leaves display a wonderful variety of shapes, colours and sizes. This one grows in my garden. The leaves do not have strong veins so it is difficult to make a good veiner from them.

Materials

Mid green flowerpaste

20- and 26-gauge white wires

Foliage green petal dust

Half glaze

Twig floristry tape

Equipment

Ivy veiner made from silicone plastique, p 8 (CS)

Ivy templates (p 155)

Scriber (PME)

1 First make the veiner from your chosen ivy leaf (page 8).

2 Roll out mid green flowerpaste, leaving a ridge to one end of the paste. Using the template, cut out the ivy leaf. Insert a moistened 26-gauge wire into the ridge, then place in the veiner to vein.

3 Remove from the veiner and soften the edges of the leaf. Place the leaves onto dimpled foam to allow them to firm up a little.

Colouring

4 Dust the ivy leaves with foliage green. For a darker result, dust before they are dry. Allow to dry.

5 Finally, dip the ivy leaves in half glaze and enhance the veins by scraping them in with the scriber. Birdsfoot ivy is made in the same way.

Weeping fig

This evergreen species (*Ficus benjamina*) can reach 20m (about 65ft) high in its native India. It is one of the most popular of all indoor plants with its tree shape, weeping habit and attractive, pendulous branches. The slender elliptical leaves are light green when young, they are approximately 10–15cm (4–6in) long, and turn a glossy green as they mature. There is also a variegated variety.

Materials

Mid and dark green flowerpaste

22- and 28-gauge white wires

Moss green and foliage green petal dusts

Half glaze

Nile green floristry tape

Equipment

Weeping fig cutters (TT 860–862) or templates (p 156)

Plain edge cutting wheel (PME)

Weeping fig veiner made from silicone plastique, p 8 (CS)

1 Roll out mid green paste, leaving a ridge at the centre. Cut out several leaf shapes using the smaller weeping fig template and the cutting wheel. Insert a moistened 28-gauge white wire into the thicker end of the ridge to about half the length of the leaf. Repeat using the darker green paste and the larger fig leaf template. Soften the edges and place in the fig leaf veiner to vein. Remove and frill the edges using a metal ball tool.

Pinch the tips to a sharp point, then place on dimpled foam to dry.

2 Dust the backs of the leaves with moss green and the front with foliage green. Dip the leaves into half glaze. Starting with smaller leaves, tape them onto a 22-gauge wire, adding a small bract to the base of each leaf stem where it meets the main stem and gradually adding further 22-gauge wires to strengthen the stem.

Pretty in Pink

We have combined the work of all three of us to create this very pretty orchid arrangement. Many of the arrangements in this book have been assembled using the method described below. *Alan, Tony and Tombi*

Flowers

5 sets of papilionanthe foliage

7 papilionanthe orchids, plus buds (p 32)

3 white vuylstekeara orchids, plus buds (p 114)

2 magenta laelia orchids, plus buds (p 84)

1 stem of deep magenta oncidium orchids with buds (p 52)

A few extra large orchid leaves

Equipment

18-gauge wire

Nile green floristry tape

Florists' staysoft (green or dark grey)

20cm (8in) diameter pewter plate

Fine-nosed pliers

Preparation

1 Strengthen any flower and foliage stems that need extra length or weight to support them by taping additional 18-gauge wire alongside the main stem. Mould a piece of staysoft onto the plate. (We have used grey staysoft to match the pewter.)

Assembly

2 As you start to include each flower stem in the arrangement, you might need to hook the end of each – this will provide further support to the stems. Start to form the basic outline of the arrangement using the papilionanthe orchid foliage. Gradually introduce some of the papilionanthe orchids to follow this basic line too.

3 Next, add the three white vuylstekeara orchids in a line straight through the centre of the arrangement. Add the buds to this line as well. Continue to add extra stems of papilionanthe orchids and foliage as you work your way through the arrangement.

4 The focal point is created using the two laelia orchids and buds – these will need to be added carefully with the aid of a pair of fine-nosed pliers to prevent breakages. Add the deep magenta oncidium orchids to add interest and more height at the back of the arrangement. Extra single flowers can be added at the base to follow the colour through.

5 Add extra foliage at the back and at the sides of the arrangement to fill in any gaps and also create a bolder image. Stand back from the display, and make any adjustments needed to 'relax' the flowers if needed.

Dreamland

A very bold design can be achieved simply with only a couple of large orchids. Here I have used some coloured skeletonized leaves to create a dream-like quality to the cake. Mexican blue flowers and foliage alongside deep magenta *Laelia* orchids create an eye-catching design. *Alan*

Cake and decoration

20cm (8in) teardrop shaped fruit cake

750g (1lb 10oz) white almond paste

750g (1lb 10oz) white sugarpaste

30cm (12in) oval cake board

Fine lilac satin ribbon

15mm lilac-purple ribbon to trim board

8 natural skeleton dyed leaves (FA)

Flowers

2 laelia orchids and buds

5 orchid leaves

3 stems of Mexican blue flowers

Equipment

20- and 24-gauge wires

Nile green floristry tape

2 fine posy picks

Preparation

1 Brush the teardrop shaped rich fruit cake with apricot glaze and cover with white almond paste. Allow the almond paste to dry for a few hours – overnight if time allows.

2 Moisten the surface of the almond paste with clear alcohol and cover with white sugarpaste. Use a pair of sugarpaste smoothers to create a neat, smooth finish.

3 A pad of sugarpaste flattened into the palm and used to polish the surface can help to produce a more flawless finish – especially with the extreme curl to the teardrop shaped cake. Cover the cake board with white sugarpaste.

4 Attach a band of fine lilac satin ribbon to the base of the cake using either a small amount of royal icing or some sugarpaste softened with clear alcohol (Kirsch, white rum or Cointreau etc).

5 Attach a band of broader lilac-purple ribbon to the edge of the cake board using a non-toxic glue stick to hold it in place.

Assembly

6 Glue a 24-gauge wire onto each of the coloured skeleton leaves using a low-melt glue-gun and non-toxic glue stick. Tape the leaves together into two groups of three, and one with two, using half width nile green floristry tape.

7 Tape together two small sprays using the laelia orchids and buds, foliage and Mexican blue flowers. Add the skeleton leaves to complete each spray.

8 As the sprays are displayed at difficult positions on the cake, it is best to insert a fine posy pick into the sides of the cake. Fill each pick with a little almond paste before adding the orchid spray.

9 Position the stem of each spray over the hole in the pick and, using a large open hook of 20-gauge wire, carefully attach each of the sprays to the pick.

10 Carefully re-arrange the orchids, skeleton leaves and foliage as necessary to hide the join between the floral sprays, cake and posy picks.

Laelia orchid

Laelia anceps, the hybrid pictured here, is native to Mexico where it is known as 'Flor de San Miguel'. It was introduced to Britain in 1834 and is one of the most important orchids in cultivation. They have been interbred with the *Cattleya* family to produce beautiful *Laeliocattleya* hybrids. Colours range from white, yellow, orange, red, lavender, pink to deep purples and brown.

Materials

White and mid green flowerpaste

18-, 22-, 24- and 26-gauge white wires

Lemon, African violet, forest green and foliage green petal dusts

Deep magenta and sap green craft dusts

Half glaze

Nile green floristry tape

Equipment

Silk veining tool (HP)

Laelia cutter set (A Priddy) or templates (p 157)

Standard amaryllis petal veiner (GI)

Tulip leaf veiner (GI)

Column

1 The column is quite small in this orchid with the lip petal tightly concealing it. Form a small ball of paste into a teardrop shape. Moisten the end of a 22-gauge white wire and insert it into the thin end of the teardrop. You will need the wire to be inserted into at least half the length of the column. Hollow out the underside of the column by simply pressing it against the length and round end of the silk veining tool. Pinch the back of the column as you do this to create a subtle ridge. Add a small ball at the tip of the column to represent the anther cap. Divide it carefully down the centre with a sharp scalpel. Allow to dry overnight (if time allows).

Labellum (lip/throat)

2 Roll out some white flowerpaste thinly, leaving the central area slightly thicker. Cut out the petal shape using the throat petal cutter. Place into the amaryllis veiner and press firmly. Remove from the veiner. Double frill the three scallops at the top of the petal using the broad end of a dresden tool. Next, soften the frilling by re-frilling, this time using the silk veining tool.

column on top of the petal and curl the side scallops over the top of the column – they can overlap or join equally at the centre depending on the variety you are making. Curl back the edges of the two side scallops, and curl the lip a little to give the flower some character. Allow to firm up a little before dusting.

Colouring

4 Dust the two ridges with lemon

26-gauge white wire into the thick ridge. Soften the edges. Vein the petal using the amaryllis petal veiner. I have frilled the edges of the wing petals slightly using the silk veining tool – there are many varieties with plain edges and some with quite flat edges too. Pinch a subtle central ridge down the centre of the petal and allow the petal to firm up with a slight curve. Repeat the same process to make two wing petals.

3 Place the petal on a pad and, using a ball tool, hollow out the two side scallops of the petal. Using a pair of plain edge angled tweezers, pinch two long ridges down the centre of the petal. Some laelia orchids have a series of fine lines in the throat: if you want to add these, it is best to paint them on at this stage using a little alcohol and your chosen colour. Apply a little egg white on either side of the petal towards the base. Place the

petal dust. I have used deep magenta craft dust to dust the main colour on the lip, with a heavy patch of African violet over the top. The lip can be the same depth of colour as the outer petals or much stronger.

Lateral petals

5 Roll out some white flowerpaste, leaving a thick ridge for the wire or using a grooved board. Cut out the wing petal shape. Insert a moistened

Dorsal sepal

6 Roll out some more white paste with a thick ridge for a fine wire. Cut out the straight dorsal sepal. Insert a moistened 26-gauge wire into half the length. Soften the edges using a medium ball tool. Vein using the amaryllis veiner, but use it upside down to create the veins tapering into the point of the petal. Pinch the sepal from the base to the tip and curve it backwards or forwards.

Lateral sepals

7 Repeat as before, but vein the sepals on the curved veins on the side of the veiner – they are not exactly curved but can be encouraged to be. Curve the sepal back slightly. Repeat to make the two sepals.

Colouring and assembly

8 Dust each petal and sepal from the base and the edges with deep magenta craft dust. Add depth from

Buds

10 Knead some white paste until pliable. Roll into a ball and then into a teardrop shape. Insert a hooked, moistened 22-gauge wire into the broad end. Divide the bud into three to represent the outer sepals of the flower. Use a scalpel, plain edge cutting wheel or a cage made with three 26-gauge wires. Give the bud a graceful curve. Dust the buds as for the flower.

create both a central vein and a ridge on the back. Allow to dry with a graceful curve.

12 Dust each leaf with forest green, fading the colour towards the edge. Overdust with sap green craft dust, and then foliage green petal dust. Dip into a half glaze. Allow to dry.

13 Tape one or two leaves onto the end of an 18-gauge wire with half

the base of each with African violet petal dust.

9 Tape the two wing petals onto either side of the throat using half width green tape. If the petals are still pliable, you will be able to create a better shape. Tape in the dorsal sepal behind the petals, and again re-adjust if required. Add the lateral sepals at the base. Tape over the stem a few times more for a fleshy stem.

Leaves

11 The leaves grow singly or in pairs from a single pseudobulb. Roll out a long sausage of mid green paste, leaving a thick ridge for the wire. Cut out a long strap-like leaf. Insert a 24- or 22-gauge wire, depending upon the size of the leaf. Place the leaf on a pad and soften the edges. Place the leaf into the tulip veiner and press firmly. Create a strong central vein by pinching the leaf firmly on the back to

width nile green floristry tape. Add a single flower or a stem with flowers and buds.

Pseudobulb

14 You will only need a pseudobulb if you are making a complete plant. Add a large ball of paste to the wire and form into a slightly ovoid shape. Divide into three sections, then pinch a ridge down the centre of each. Dust and glaze as for the leaves.

Mexican blue flower

The 50 *Lisianthius* species are a group of woody and shrub-like gentians from South America and the West Indies. *Lisianthius nigrescens* from Mexico is commonly known as 'Flor de Muerto' because it is a favoured as a decoration for graves in southern Mexico. I have re-named it for use in this book. The flowers can be an even darker blue-black than I have made them here!

Materials
White and mid green flowerpaste
26-gauge wire
Five-petal calyx cutter (R12)
Purple and Prussian blue craft dusts
Vine, foliage, forest and edelweiss petal dusts
Nile green floristry tape
Plain edge cutting wheel (PME)

1 For buds, form white paste into a teardrop shape and insert a hooked, moistened 26-gauge wire into the base. Pinch the base onto the wire and work it to create an elongated bud. Divide the tip into five.

2 For flowers, form white paste into a long slender teardrop shape. Pinch out the broad end. Thin out the base using a small celstick. Cut out the flower shape using the calyx cutter. Elongate each petal using a rolling action. Open up the flower centre using the pointed end of the celstick. Pinch each petal to create a central vein. Curl edges back slightly. Dust the flowers and buds with a mixture of purple and blue, leaving the centre paler. Add vine green at the centre.

3 For the calyx, twist a length of quarter width tape back on itself to

form a thin strand. Make five strands for each flower and bud. Tape around the base. Dust with vine and foliage petal dusts.

4 For the leaves, roll out green paste, leaving a thick ridge for the wire. Cut a leaf shape. Insert a moistened 26-gauge wire into the thick ridge. Soften the edge, then pinch a central vein from the base to of the leaf. Dust with a little forest green and overdust with edelweiss and foliage mixed. Tape the flowers into groups, adding the leaves in pairs where they join the main stem.

Sunburst Splendour

This stunning wedding cake, adorned with bright orange orchids and an exotic passionflower, is perfect for a couple planning to marry on a tropical beach or as a colourful reminder of the happy event at a reception back home. Just one vibrantly coloured passionflower is enough. *Tombi*

Cake and decoration

30cm (12in) oval cake

30cm (12in) long oval cake

1.25kg (2¾lb) white almond paste

1.75kg (3¾lb) ivory sugarpaste

40cm (16in) oval and long oval boards

Ivory ribbon to trim cake and board

Flowers

3 sprays passionflower 'Sunburst' leaves, plus 2 large leaves

4 passionflower 'Sunburst' buds

2 sprays comparettia speciosa orchids

1 passionflower 'Sunburst'

Equipment

No. 1 piping tube (tip) (optional)

Large posy pick

1 'Tombi' tilted perspex separator (CC)

Preparation

1 Brush the cakes with apricot glaze and cover with almond paste. Cover the cake boards with sugarpaste. Use the tin the cakes were baked in to carefully remove the sugarpaste from the centres of the boards where the cakes will be placed. Leave to dry. Moisten the surface of the almond paste with clear alcohol and cover the cakes with sugarpaste. Smooth the surface with smoothers and set aside to dry.

2 Use a non-toxic glue stick or double-sided sticky tape to attach the ribbon to the cake board edges. Fasten the ribbon around the base of the cakes. If liked, using a No. 1 piping tube (tip), pipe a snail's trail around the base of the cakes using sugarpaste softened to a piping consistency with Grand Marnier.

Assembly

3 Tape up the three leaf sprays onto 18-gauge wires, starting the sprays with small leaves and buds increasing the size of the leaves towards to end. Add loose looking tendrils to the front end of the sprays (when the tendrils make contact with a support

they then tighten into the spiral shape). The three leaf sprays should be of varying lengths (each about 40cm (16in), 33cm (13in) and 25cm (10in) long).

4 Tape the two sprays of orchids onto the two longer passionflower leaf sprays, then tape the shorter leaf spray between the two longer pieces, allowing a good length of stem tape in the passionflower. Tape in the two large passionflower leaves to cover the join and pull in the passionflower.

5 Cut off the excess wires and finish off the end of the spray neatly with tape, making sure it will fit into the posy pick.

6 Insert the end of the spray into the large posy pick and, supporting the leaf sprays, carefully insert the posy pick into the long oval cake two-thirds of the way down the cake and to the side.

7 Place the separator at an angle on the oval cake and arrange the narrower cake at an attractive angle. Stand back and make the final adjustments to the arrangement.

Comparettia speciosa

This genus takes its name from the Italian botanist A. Comparetti. It consists of about twelve kinds of small epiphytic orchids and is found in the Andes. Small bulbs, long stalks, lateral sepals forming a long spur and large dense clusters of flowers are the main characteristics of this genus.

Materials
Pale green and melon flowerpaste
18-, 24-, 26- and 28-gauge white wires
Nasturtium, primrose, vine green, red and leaf green petal dusts
Nile green floristry tape

Equipment
Medium column mould (optional) (HH)
Cutters (TT 543, 737) or template (p 156)
Stargazer (B) veiner (GI)
Needle frilling tool (CC)

Column
1 Roll a small piece of very pale green paste into a ball and insert it onto the end of a moistened half length 24-gauge wire. Form into a carrot shape and place in the mould. Roll a metal ball tool from the wire up to the tip of the column. Pinch the tip to a sharp point. Ensure it is very curved.

Petals and sepal
2 Roll out a piece of melon paste over a groove, moisten a quarter length 28-gauge wire and place it along the groove. Roll the wire into the paste; fold the paste over the wire, sandwiching it. Roll out the paste again. Place the cutter over the wire, with the square end at the edge of the board. Cut out the shape. Vein the shape, place on a foam pad and lightly flute the edge with a ball tool. Work the edge gently with the needle frilling tool.

3 Run down the centre of the shape with a dresden tool to vein it. Gently pull back on the tip of the sepal to curve it. Set aside until leather hard. The two lateral petals are made in exactly the same way.

Labellum (lip/throat)

4 Cut out the lip from melon paste and insert a moistened third length 26-gauge wire into the thickened centre. Place the lip in the veiner and

Bud

5 Form the paste into a long 'tadpole' shape, inserting a length of hooked, moistened 24-gauge wire through the thick part of the paste. Pinch to attach. Mark three lines onto the head. Tape with nile green tape.

Colouring and assembly

6 As the lip in particular is a strong colour, dust with the nasturtium petal dust (to which a little red has been

onto the petals and sepal. Paint orangy/red lines onto the lip, fading towards the lip.

Assembly

8 Dust the underneath part of the column with a mixture of leaf and vine green dusts. Dust the back of the column lightly with vine green.

9 Tape the column, lip, petals and sepals tightly, continuing to the ends

vein it. Work the edge of the petal with the needle frilling tool. Press the tip of the petal firmly with a dresden tool. Form a square shape at either side of the wire at the top of the lip. Vein the centre of the lip strongly with the dresden tool. Use a celstick or smooth porcelain tool to shape the petals attractively, accentuating the indentation at the bottom of the lip by encouraging it to curve backwards. Dry until leather hard.

added) to get a strong colour to the petal. Add some primrose to the lip where the wire is inserted into the petal and on either side create a protrusion, add some vine green petal dust. Allow to dry.

7 Dust a little nasturtium dust onto the tips of the petals and sepal, and a little vine green and slightly more primrose from the wire upwards. When dry, paint parallel orange lines

of the wire. Bend the stem of the orchid using pliers. Roll a long, fine piece of pale green flowerpaste, dust lightly with vine green, then moisten the end and attach this to the wire immediately behind the lip. Curve the spur into an attractive shape. (It is much easier to dust the spur before it is added to the orchid.)

10 Tape buds and then flowers to an 18-gauge wire.

Passionflower 'Sunburst'

I saw this beautiful *Passiflora* 'Sunburst' on the cover of a gardening magazine. It was just what I needed to go with the very bold *Comparettia speciosa*, a marriage made in heaven. I made veiners from the leaves of a red banana passionflower acquired from a butterfly farm as I preferred them to the more common passionflower. There were no leaves in the illustration of this amazing passionflower.

Materials

18-, 20-, 24-, 26-, 28- and 33-gauge wires
Pale green, mid green, yellow and white flowerpaste
Yellow Sugartex or yellow pollen dust
Small round, white stamens
Primrose, vine green, African violet, deep purple, nasturtium, red, egg yellow, holly/ivy, edelweiss, nutkin brown and leaf green petal dusts
Quarter glaze
Nile green floristry tape

Equipment

Cutters (TT 457, 723–725) or templates (p 156)
Protea petal cutters (SC)
Stargazer (B) veiner (GI)
Plain edge cutting wheel (PME)
Red banana passionflower leaf veiners made from silicone plastique, p 8 (CS)
Needle frilling tool (CC)

Pistil and Stamens

1 Cut a 28-gauge wire into three. Thread a small ball of pale green paste onto the wire, work it up the wire and take it slightly over the tip. Place the end of the paste on a pad and use a small ball tool to cup it neatly. Curve into a lazy S shape.

2 Bend the end of a 28-gauge wire into the shape of a seven. Roll a small

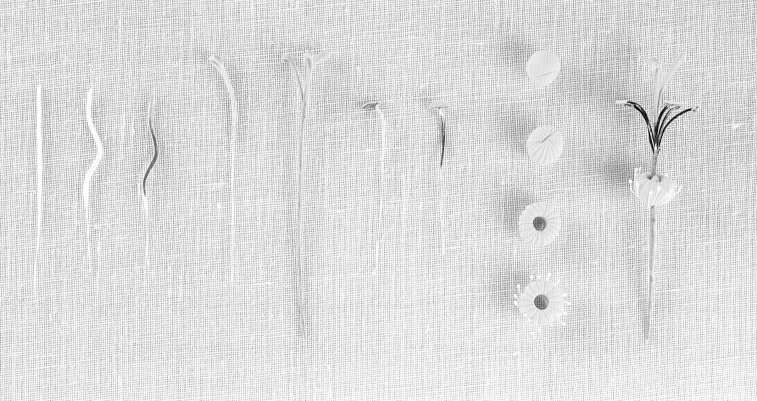

piece of mid green paste into a short grain shape. Moisten the bent piece of the wire and insert into the middle of the grain. Fasten it on securely with your fingers. Curve the shape slightly. Moisten the top and dip into yellow Sugartex or yellow pollen dust. Set aside. When it is dry, thread a tiny ball of flowerpaste below the T bar shape and work the paste onto the wire, keeping it very slender. Make five of these.

Centre
3 Roll a medium sized piece of yellow paste into a round ball. Push a medium sized celstick into the middle and use the cutting wheel to mark many grooves onto the side of the 'donut' shape. Remove from the medium sized celstick and enlarge the centre with a larger celstick. Continue the grooves into the centre of the 'donut'. While the paste is still soft, mix up some 'gunge' (mix some

flowerpaste and egg white together to make a very sticky glue). Cut the round headed stamens into short lengths and stick them into the grooves (about every second or third groove). Set aside to dry completely.

Filaments
4 Cut twelve 33- or 35-gauge wires into quarters, thread a tiny ball of yellow paste onto a moistened wire and work the paste onto the wire

until very slender. Bend into a very shallow lazy S before it hardens. The paste on the filaments should be half the length of the shorter petal cutter.

Petals

5 Roll out pale green paste over a groove, lay a moistened 26-gauge third length wire along the groove. Roll it in, fold back the paste, roll out again and cut out a shape with one of the two sizes of petal cutters.

the centre. It does not need to be enlarged in the centre. Cut out a shape using the calyx cutter. Vein the shape with the stargazer (B) veiner. Place the calyx on a foam pad and cup each sepal without removing the veining. Very carefully work the edge with the tip of a dresden tool (not the veiner end). If you look at the buds of a passionflower carefully they have little 'hooks' rather like Velcro along the edge of the sepals.

10 Dust the centre 'donut' with primrose petal dust in the centre, nasturtium and red on the outside, being very careful to colour the stamens as well, without knocking them off!

11 Dust the filaments with the primrose yellow petal dust at the tip, add egg yellow petal dust, then nasturtium petal dust which goes to the end. Dust the end of the

6 Dust the stargazer (B) veiner and vein the petal. Place on a piece of foam and hook the tip of the petal with a metal ball tool. Slide your fingers along the outside of the petal to make it curve inwards slightly. Repeat this process ten times, five of each of the two cutter sizes.

Calyx

7 Make a second much smaller 'donut' and mark it the same way as

Dusting and assembly

8 Tape the three pieces which form the pistil onto the end of a two-thirds length 18-gauge wire. Dust them with primrose and vine green dusts.

9 Add the five stamens below the pistil, arranging them evenly around the centre. Moisten some of the African violet and deep purple dust and colour the filaments. Tape down the stem for about 5cm (2in).

flowerpaste nearest the wire with a little vine green petal dust. Dust a small amount of red over the nasturtium petal dust.

12 Put the 18-gauge wire, holding the pistil and stamens, through the centre of the centre 'donut' and tape the filaments tightly behind it. When they are firmly bedded, stick the donut to the filaments with some of the gunge.

13 Dust the petals with holly/ivy petal dust near the wire, lightening to vine green petal dust, and then dust some edelweiss petal dust from the hooked tip.

14 Tape these petals tightly behind the filaments. Tape down the wire for about 5cm (2in). Dust the second, smaller donut with egg yellow petal dust, then stick behind the petals with some gunge.

15 Dust the calyx with egg yellow petal dust and a little nasturtium petal dust, and carefully colour the 'Velcro' edges with nutkin brown petal dust. Moisten the centre and thread the 18-gauge wire through the centre. Hang the calyx upside down for a short while for it to set in place. When the calyx is set, dust the central 'donut' with a final finishing touch of mixed African violet and deep purple dusts.

16 Thicken the stem of the passionflower with nile green tape. Steam the flower to set the dust.

Buds

17 Make the buds exactly as described for the calyx, but attach them to an oval piece of paste which has been attached onto third length moistened and hooked 24-gauge wire. Moisten the edges of the calyx and close carefully so that the worked edges are just touching one another to make an attractive bud. Dust with some egg yellow, nasturtium and nutkin brown dust. Steam to set.

Leaves

18 Make a number of leaves, using a grooved board and the red banana passionflower veiner (or something similar). Work the edge of the leaves first with a dresden tool, then gently with a frilling needle and finally roll a

ball tool over the edge to soften the working on a foam pad. Dust the leaves with leaf green and vine green, overdusting with holly/ivy petal dust. Allow to dry completely. Dip into quarter glaze and, while the glaze is still soft, use a scriber to scratch in lighter veins.

19 Tape the leaves onto an 18-gauge wire, adding a dusted 33-gauge wire in loose curls for the tendrils. The tendrils only spiral into the familiar 'spring' shape when they have latched onto something to lift the branch on. The lifting is done by the tendrils tightening into spirals.

20 Tape three sprays of leaves together, adding buds and tendrils attractively as you proceed. Add the flower to the centre. Stand back, adjust if necessary, then take time to admire your work!

Garnet Glory

This striking garnet coloured arrangement has great visual power and passion. The rich red *Burrageara* orchids have been entwined with weeping fig leaves (page 79) to make a stunning arrangement inserted into the knot of a piece of driftwood. The buds of this beautiful orchid are particularly fascinating during the opening stages. First, the tips remain closed with the sepals becoming separated then, very suddenly, the tip loosens during a power surge of growth and the flower is completely open. *Tony*

Burrageara orchid

Burrageara 'Nelly Isler' orchid is a perfect example of a completely man-made genus. This has been achieved by cross-breeding *Miltonia*, *Cochlioda*, *Odontoglossum* and *Oncidium* orchids. The end result is an eye-catching family of light and rich dark red orchids that make wonderful flowers which would be suitable for Christmas, ruby wedding or valentine cakes.

Materials

White, pale ruby (with a little claret food colouring added), dark ruby and mid green flowerpaste

18-, 20-, 22-, 24-, 26- and 28-gauge white wires

Ruby red paste colour

Ruby, lemon yellow, burgundy, vine green, moss and forest green petal dusts

Half glaze

Nile green floristry tape

Equipment

Orchid column mould made from silicone plastique, p 8 (CS)

Burrageara orchid cutters (TT 864–867) or templates (p 157)

Burrageara orchid veiners

Plain edge cutting wheel (PME)

Stipple brush

Fine paintbrush

Column

1 Make a mould from silicone plastique using a real orchid (page 8). Roll a small amount of white flowerpaste into a sausage shape, insert a moistened 24-gauge wire and place into the mould to form the column. (This will only need a very small amount of flowerpaste.)

2 Or, roll a small amount of white flowerpaste into a sausage shape, insert a moistened 24-gauge wire, hollow out the underside using a dresden tool, then flute either side and cup a small anther cap on the end of the column. Do not make the column too long otherwise it will not fit the labellum.

Labellum (lip/throat)

3 Roll out pale ruby flowerpaste (see Materials), leaving a ridge down the centre. Cut out a lip using the lip

the edge of the petal in the same direction as the veins in the petals, then place on dimpled foam to dry.

Lateral petals

6 Roll out dark ruby flowerpaste, leaving a ridge in the centre of the paste (you might prefer to use a grooved board for this).

7 Cut out a petal using the wing petal cutter. Insert a moistened a 28-

Dorsal and lateral sepals

8 Repeat the previous lateral petal instructions to make the three outer sepals, using the appropriate cutters and veiners.

Colouring

9 Mix ruby petal dust with clear alcohol and, using a stipple brush, load the brush with the colour, trying not to get too much on the brush at one time.

cutter or the template on page 157. Insert a moistened 26-gauge wire into the ridge.

4 Place a small piece of flowerpaste into the dip in the lip veiner to form the raised platform.

5 Soften the edges of the lip petal and place in the veiner. Remove from veiner and place edge of the lip on your finger. Using a cocktail stick, roll

gauge wire into the central ridge of the petal, holding the thick ridge firmly between your finger and thumb to prevent the wire piercing through the petal. Place the petal onto a pad and soften the edges using a medium ball tool. Vein the petal using the wing petal veiner. Press the veiner firmly to give slightly stronger veining. Pinch the petal at the base and the tip slightly and allow to firm up over some dimpled foam.

10 Holding the lip in one hand and the brush in the other, pull back the bristles with your thumb and release the bristles to flick some tiny spots and speckles onto the lip, giving a more natural appearance. You will need to flick more colour at the centre and base of the petal to create a denser look.

11 Mix a little ruby red paste colour with clear alcohol and paint lines using a fine paintbrush either side from the base of the raised platform. Next, paint the raised platform with lemon yellow petal dust mixed with clear alcohol, and finally paint three very fine lines down the raised platform using ruby red paste colour mixed again with a little alcohol.

12 Dust the petals and sepals with ruby petal dust and then overdust the centres of each with burgundy petal

Steam the flower very lightly to set the colour.

Buds
14 Half open buds are made in the same way as the open orchid, but instead of drying the petals curving back, curve them inwards so that when they are taped together the tips of each petal will meet – this will give a much more realistic look to the finished bud.

a light overdusting of moss green petal dust.

Assembly
17 Tape approximately five or six buds in various sizes onto an 18-gauge wire with half width nile green floristry tape. Alternate the buds as you work down the stem, adding a bract to each bud as it joins the main stem. These are made from small strips of floristry tape. Add a half

dust, and the base of each with lemon yellow petal dust. Dust the top of column with very lightly with ruby petal dust.

Assembly
13 Tape the column to the lip using half width nile green floristry tape. Add the two lateral petals onto either side of the column and lip. Tape in the dorsal sepal behind the lateral petals and finally two lateral sepals.

15 Make the small buds in various sizes by rolling pale ruby colour flowerpaste into a cigar shape. Pinch the sides to divide into three and coax them into a sharp point to the tip, bending them over slightly. Insert a 26-gauge moistened hooked wire into the broad end of the bud.

16 Dust the buds with vine green petal dust, then ruby and burgundy petal dusts. Dust the small buds with

open bud and then about two or three open flowers, each with a bract where they join the main stem.

Leaves
18 The leaves are long and strap-like, growing from both the centre and the sides of a round to ovoid shaped pseudobulb. I have made my own veiner for the leaf using silicone plastique and a leaf from the actual plant (page 8). Alternatively, a long

tulip leaf veiner may be used. Roll out a long strip of well kneaded mid green flowerpaste, leaving a thick ridge down the length to insert a wire. Cut out the leaf shape using the large end of the plain edge cutting wheel.

19 Supporting the thick ridge firmly between your finger and thumb, insert a moistened 22- or 20-gauge wire, depending upon the size of the

leaf. Take the leaf out of the veiner and pinch a good central vein and ridge onto the back of the leaf. Then allow the leaf to firm up slightly before colouring.

21 The leaves grow in pairs from the pseudobulb. You will need to make two leaves, dust them and allow them to dry thoroughly. The remainder of the foliage is made just before you assemble a leaf group, as

an 18-gauge wire with half width nile green floristry tape. Attach a ball of paste at the base to represent the pseudobulb. Pinch the ball tightly onto the base of the leaves – this will create a more ovoid shaped bulb. Pinch the two sides of the bulb slightly and then texture with a series of fine lines, created using a sharp scalpel or the plain edge cutting wheel. Dust the pseudobulb lightly as for the leaves.

leaf. The wire should be inserted about half way up the ridge to give it support.

20 Place the leaf onto a pad and, using a medium metal ball tool, soften the edges slightly to remove the cut edge appearance. Carefully position the leaf into either the homemade veiner or the tulip leaf veiner and squeeze the two sides together firmly to make a good impression on the

they need to be taped and stuck down tightly against the pseudobulb at the base of the two dried central leaves.

22 Dust the leaves lightly with forest green petal dust. Overdust with foliage and moss green. Dip into a half glaze. Allow to dry.

Pseudobulb
23 Tape the two dried leaves onto

Assembly
24 Tape a stem of orchids to the pinched side of the pseudobulb. While the other leaves are still slightly pliable, tape them in pairs, one on either side of the pseudobulb. Keep adding further sets of leaves until you have created the desired look.

25 To create a growing plant, place staysoft into a plant pot to secure the stem. See also page 129.

Grace

I named this pretty cake after my youngest grand-daughter, Grace. It seemed suitable to make it a Christening cake as she had recently been christened. Adorned with two kinds of attractive pink orchids, it would also make a beautiful Mother's Day cake. *Tombi*

Cake and decoration
20cm (8in) teardrop fruit cake
1kg (2¼lb) white almond paste
1.5kg (3¼lb) white sugarpaste
25cm (10in) round cake board
Pink ribbon to trim cake and board
50g (2oz) pink flowerpaste
Pink pearl lustre colour

Flowers
3 sprays of Portuguese fern (step 5)
1 spray of epidendrum prismatocarpum
orchids with buds
3 sprays of encyclia sima orchids

Equipment
Mini orchid mould (HH)
Small glass jar
Florists' staysoft

Preparation
1 Brush the cake with apricot glaze and cover with almond paste. Cover the cake board with sugarpaste. Use the tin the cake was baked in to carefully remove the sugarpaste from the centre of the board where the cake will be placed. Leave to dry. Moisten the surface with clear alcohol and lift the sugarpaste over the cake. Smooth the surface with smoothers.

2 Place the cake onto the board. Attach the ribbon around the base of the cake to neaten the edge. Attach the ribbon to the edge of the board.

Side design
3 Mix together equal amounts of flowerpaste and sugarpaste and leave for 2 hours. Break off pieces of the paste, roll into a smooth ball, dust with cornflour and push into the orchid mould. Make an equal number of the four orchid types, Leave to dry until leather hard.

4 When leather hard, attach them around the ribbon with royal icing. Carry one through onto the board and one onto the edge of the cake.

Portuguese fern
5 Roll out pale green flowerpaste across a groove, moisten a third length 28- or 26-gauge wire and place it along the groove. Roll the wire into the paste. Fold back the paste, sandwiching it, and roll out again. Cut out the leaf using a Portuguese fern cutter (CS 889, 890) or template (p 156). Vein the leaf with a No. 27 veiner (CC) and work each notch with a silk veining tool. Accentuate some frilling with a frilling tool. When dry, dust one side with vine green and the other with chestnut petal dust. Overdust the leaf with holly/ivy. Steam to set. Tape the leaves alternately onto 18-gauge wire to form stems.

Assembly
6 Fill the glass jar with staysoft. Arrange the epidendrum prismatocarpum, encyclia sima and Portuguese fern sprays into the staysoft, tall enough to show above the cake. Place the container into the curve of the teardrop and arrange attractively over and to one side of the cake.

7 Tape together a smaller spray of the encyclia orchids and foliage, then display on the board on the opposite side of the cake from the arrangement. Dust both of the orchids with pink pearl lustre colour.

Encyclia sima

This is one of the group sometimes known as 'cockleshell orchids'. They are more tender than the tougher Mexican varieties. *Encyclia sima* is only found in the cloud forest near the summit of a mountain in central Panama. It was first described as recently as 1969. Its flowers are produced in spring and are highly fragrant. The leaves are broad, dark olive green with a paler vein down the centre.

Materials

Very pale pink flowerpaste

24- and 28-gauge white wires

Deep magenta craft dust mixed with edelweiss petal dust to give a pale pink dust

Primrose petal dust

Ruby and purple liquid food colours

Nile green floristry tape

Equipment

Column mould (medium) (HH)

Cutters (TT 543, 801, 802) or templates (p 156)

Stargazer (B) veiner (GI)

Needle frilling tool (CC)

Very fine paintbrush

Column

1 Take a small piece of pink paste and roll it into a small ball. Moisten the end of a third length 24-gauge wire and fasten the ball to it. Put the ball into the front end of a column mould. Roll a ball tool up the wire to cup the column, then curve the wire and cut off the excess. Pinch a point to the tip of the column. Press a small ball tool into the centre of the underside of the column to make it round.

Labellum (lip/throat)

2 Roll a piece of pink paste over a groove, moisten a third length 28-gauge wire and lay it along the groove. Roll the wire into the paste, then fold back the excess paste, sandwiching the wire. Roll out again. Place the cutter (543) over the rolled out paste – the square end should be level with the end of the board, the wire should extend about half way down the petal. Cut out the shape.

pad and soften the edges of the petals without frilling them. Curve the petals backwards. Put aside to dry.

Dorsal sepal

5 Roll out paste, inserting a quarter length 28-gauge wire almost to the tip of the petal. Cut it out with cutter No. 802; vein the petal as before. If you were aiming to create a more realistic orchid, you would run a ball tool down the centre of the

Assembly and decoration

7 Dust a little of the pink dust onto the back of the column and onto the widest part of the lip petal.

8 Dust primrose onto the inside and side edges of the column and onto the pollen guides.

9 Using a very fine brush, paint parallel lines of dark purple/red lines onto the lip. Allow to dry.

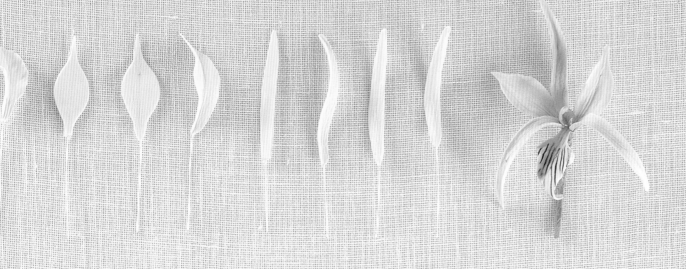

3 Dust the veiner and vein the petal. Frill the edge of the petal with the needle frilling tool and curl the petal down and back. Pinch two lines on either side of the wire to form the pollen guides. Put aside to set,

Lateral petals

4 Repeat the process described for the lip in step 2 but using cutter No. 801. Dust the veiner with cornflour and vein the petal. Place onto a foam

underside of the petal to make it cup backwards before bending it into a lazy S bend; I have veined the petal between my fingers before bending to shape. Dry.

Lateral sepals

6 Repeat as for the dorsal sepal until the shaping. The lateral sepals are bent into a C shape rather than a lazy S, and the same comment is made regarding realistic petals. Dry.

10 Tape the column tightly to the labellum – the column almost touches the labellum. Add the two lateral petals, then add the lateral sepals and lastly the dorsal sepal. Pull down on each wire to check that it is very tightly bedded before taping down the stem.

11 The buds for this orchid are long and slender with strong lines between the sepals.

Epidendrum prismatocarpum

Epidendrum is a very large genus; some specialists say there are over five hundred species. The genus also covers both epiphytic and terrestrial species, some from South and Central America and others from the veld of Africa. This particular *Epidendrum prismatocarpum is* from Panama. They are epiphytic, medium scented flowers with narrow white petals and a pinky purplish lip. Good orchids for cross breeding, they blossom before the other species.

Materials

White and pale pink flowerpaste
24- and 26-gauge white wires
Primrose, vine green and edelweiss petal dusts
Deep magenta craft dust
Nile green floristry tape

Equipment

Medium column mould
Cutters (TT 666, 804, 805) or templates (p 156)
Needle frilling tool (CC)
Silk veining tool (HP)
Fine, curved scissors
Stargazer (B) veiner (GI)

Column

1 Roll a small piece of white paste into a ball and push it onto the moistened tip of a 24-gauge wire. Roll into a carrot shape, then place in the mould. Roll a metal ball tool up the column, cupping the column, curving the wire, cutting off excess. Pinch the tip of the column to a point. Dry.

Labellum (lip/throat)

2 Roll out a piece of pink paste over

a groove, moisten a third length of 26-gauge wire along the groove, fold back the paste, sandwiching the wire, roll out again. Cut out the shape.

3 Use the frilling needle to broaden the neck end of the lip slightly. Work the edge of the petal very well with the silk veining tool, keeping the veins parallel with the edge of the cutter. Reinforce the frilling using the frilling needle. On some of these lips, the

white paste and place a moistened third length 26-gauge wire down the length of the groove. The wire should almost go to the tip of the petal. Fold back the paste and roll out again. Cut out the shape. Dust the veiner with cornflour and vein each sepal. Place the sepal on the palm of your hand and gently roll a metal ball tool from the tip to the wire. This will both cup the petal and curve the wire. Leave to dry.

the bud. Make a cage with a piece of 24-gauge wire and groove the bud. If you prefer, you can create the groove with a plain edge cutting wheel.

Colouring and assembly
7 Dust the pollen guides and the spikes with primrose dust. Dust the underside of the column a light or deep purply pink. Dust the pink on either side of the pollen guides and down towards the edge of the petal.

edges of the petal curl sharply backwards, but a few form a slight shovel shape – I prefer these. Vein down the centre of the petal with a dresden tool. Pinch a line on either side of the wire at the top of the petal and, using the scissors, cut two spikes at the back of the petal. Dry.

Dorsal and lateral sepals
4 The dorsal and lateral sepals are worked in the same way. Roll out

5 Repeat the process as in step 4 but this time use the shorter cutter to cut the lateral petals. Repeat the rest of the process. Set aside to dry.

Buds
6 The buds are long slender buds with a long throat. Roll a piece of paste onto the end of a third length 24-gauge wire, form a point and then work the paste down the wire. Work the paste more firmly for the 'neck' of

8 Moisten dust with clear alcohol and paint in some stronger lines of colour onto the dusted pink of the lip. Dust the base of the buds (and some smaller buds) with vine green.

9 Tape the column directly over the lip, tape in the lateral petals, the lateral sepals and finally the dorsal sepal. Pull down each wire to make sure it is firmly bedded. Tape down the stem and steam the flower.

Purple Rain

Orchids are often very bold flowers in both colour and form so it is very easy to use them by themselves in floral arrangements. Here I have used eye-catching purple lipped *Lemboglossum* orchids in a very striking arrangement in a glass vase with tiny purple stones and broken shells. The majority of the orchids and foliage have been used above and around the vase, but I have used some inside the vase to create added interest. *Alan*

Lemboglossum orchid

Lemboglossum orchids were originally classified under the genus *Odontoglossum*, however over the years, taxonomists have re-classified nearly all the *Odontoglossum* orchids collected from north of the Panama Isthmus to northern Mexico as *Lemboglossum*. There are about 14 species of *Lemboglossum* with many more hybrid varieties.

Materials
18-, 22-, 26-, 28- and 30-gauge wires
White and mid green flowerpaste
Cyclamen liquid colour (SK)
Lemboglossum orchid cutters
(TT 766-768) or templates (p 153)
Amaryllis petal veiner (GI) or similar
Primrose, vine green, edelweiss, aubergine,
African violet, forest and foliage green
petal dusts with deep magenta craft dust
Tulip leaf veiner
Half glaze

Column
1 Insert a 30-gauge white wire into a small ball of white paste. Work the paste down the wire between your finger and thumb, leaving the tip of the column more bulbous. Press the column against the length and round end of a ceramic tool to hollow out the length. Thin the bulbous end edges. Curve the column and pinch a gentle ridge down the back. Paint tiny spots using cyclamen colour onto the underside.

Labellum (lip/throat)
2 Roll out white paste, leaving a thick ridge. Cut out the throat petal and insert a moistened 26-gauge white wire into the ridge. Work out a 'flap' either side of the petal base.

3 Vein the petal using the amaryllis veiner. Place the petal against your index finger and frill against it using a silk veining tool. Create two fine ridges down the petal centre. Pinch the petal from the base to the tip. Encourage the two 'flaps' to stand up on either side of the petal. Add a raised platform at the base of petal by attaching a tiny ball of paste divided into two. Support the petal around the wire and then bend the lip forwards slightly. Dust the platform with primrose petal dust. The lip colour will depend on the particular variety. Fade the colour out towards the petal edges.

Colouring and assembly

5 Dust the outer petals/sepals with vine green and edelweiss mixed. Paint freehand stripes onto the back and front of each petal using a fine brush and cyclamen. Allow to dry, then dust the petal/sepal edges with aubergine and African violet mix. Tape the column onto the throat petal using half width tape. Add the wing petals onto either side of the throat, then add the three sepals.

Buds

6 Roll a ball of paste into a sharp

Leaves

7 Roll out mid green paste, leaving a thick ridge. Cut out the leaf shape. Insert a moistened 22-gauge wire into about half the length. Soften the edges. Vein using the tulip leaf veiner. Pinch the leaf from the base to the tip for a strong central vein on the front. Dust with forest and foliage green. Dry, then dip into half glaze.

Assembly

8 Start with a small bud taped onto the end of an 18-gauge wire. Alternate the buds then flowers.

Outer petals and sepals

4 Roll out white paste thinly, leaving a thick ridge down the centre. Cut out a petal/sepal shape. Insert a moistened 30-gauge white wire. Soften the edges. Pinch the petal from the base to the tip to create a central vein. Repeat to make two petals and three sepals. The dorsal sepal should be slightly cupped and dried curving forwards. The other petals/sepals are dried curving back.

pointed bud shape. Insert a hooked, moistened 26- or 28-gauge white wire into the broader end of the bud. Divide the bud into three to represent the three outer sepals. Pinch each sepal down the centre to create a ridge on each – this gives the buds an angular appearance. Curve the whole bud slightly. Repeat to make several buds in graduating sizes. Dust and paint the buds as for the outer petals/sepals of the flower.

graduating in size down the stem. Add some tiny bracts at the base of each flower and bud – optional.

9 Add extra 18-gauge wire to the stem and add two leaves at the base. For the ovoid pseudobulb, add a large ball of green paste at the base and mould into shape. Pinch either side of the bulb to create two gentle ridges. Add a series of fine lines. Dust as for leaves. Dry, then dip into half glaze.

Infanta

I thought these *Vuylstekeara* orchids would make a very attractive decoration for a Christening cake, with the dainty bouvardia adding to the delicacy of the arrangement. Those of us who make cakes with flower arrangements on them are continually looking for different containers or candle holders; I thought this tilted candle holder would work well. *Tombi*

Cake and decoration

20cm (8in) round cake

850g (1lb 14oz) white almond paste

1kg (2¼lb) white sugarpaste

28cm (11in) round cake board

Narrow white ribbon to trim cake

White ribbon to trim board

Flowers

5 vuylstekeara orchids and buds

3 sprays of birdsfoot ivy, two short and one longer (p 78) – TT 750–752

7 clusters of bouvardia flowers and foliage

Equipment

18-gauge wire

Florists' staysoft

Large and medium posy picks

Tilted candle holder or stand

Preparation

1 Brush the cake with apricot glaze, cover with almond paste and leave to dry. Moisten the outer edge of the cake board with clear alcohol and cover the board with sugarpaste. Use the tin the cake was baked in as a template to cut out a circle of sugarpaste from the centre.

2 Moisten the almond paste with clear alcohol and drape the sugarpaste carefully over the cake. Smooth over with smoothers to complete a perfect finish. Leave to dry, then position on the board.

3 Attach the narrow white ribbon around the base of the cake with royal icing. Use a glue stick to attach the ribbon to the edge of the board.

4 Carefully cut through the sugarpaste where you want to insert the large posy pick and cut out some of the cake, if necessary.

Assembly

5 Start wiring up the curving spray by wiring together some of the vuylstekeara buds. Add a short stem of birdsfoot ivy leaves just behind the buds. Add the first orchid, then a spray of bouvardia behind and in front of the orchid. Tape in the next orchid, adding further sprays of bouvardia. Add the final orchid and the final spray of bouvardia and the longer stem of ivy leaves. Insert the stem of the arrangement into the large posy pick and, holding the pick with a pair of pliers, insert it into the cake side edge. Ensure the posy pick remains slightly proud so that it can seen when cutting the cake.

6 If you wish to insert the spray to the front of the cake into a posy pick, then the orchids, bouvardia and birdsfoot ivy sprays should all be taped together so that they will fit into the pick. Carefully, insert the posy pick into the side of the cake at an angle – see step 4.

7 If using a candle holder instead of a pick, fill it with staysoft and simply push the arrangement into it, making sure the staysoft is well hidden.

8 If wished, pipe the Christening date and baby's name on the cake.

Vuylstekeara orchid

Vuylstekeara orchids are multi-generic orchids created by Charles Vuylsteke (1844–1927) who had an orchid nursery in Belgium where he crossed *Cochlioda*, *Miltonia* and *Odontoglossom* to get this beautiful hybrid. One of the most popular orchids is a red and white *Vuylstekeara* named 'Cambria Plush'. It is the rich colouring and the fact that the flowers bloom through the year that make it so popular.

Materials

White flowerpaste
18-, 24-, 26- and 28-gauge white wires
Deep magenta craft dust
Deep purple and egg yellow petal dusts
Nile green floristry tape

Equipment

Dendrobium orchid column mould (HH)
Orchid cutters (TT 440, 806–809)
(optional) or templates (p 157)
Vuylstekeara veiners made from silicone
plastique, Stargazer (B) veiner (GI) or ivy
varigator cutter
Needle frilling tool (CC)
Silk veining tool (HP)

Column

1 Take a very small piece of white flowerpaste and roll it into a ball, then into a carrot shape. Insert a moistened half length 24-gauge wire into the ball and fasten it on. Place the carrot into the column mould and roll a small metal ball tool up the wire. This will cup and curve the column at the same time. Remove the excess paste. Pinch out two 'wings' on either side of the column lip and

extend them slightly. Before the
column is dry, dust with deep
magenta and a little deep purple dust.
Set aside to dry completely. When
dry, steam to set the dust.

Labellum (lip/throat)

2 Roll out a piece of white paste
over a groove, moisten a third length
26-gauge wire and stick it onto the
paste along the groove. Fold back the
paste, sandwiching the wire, roll out

the paste again and cut out the lip
shape using the cutter. Dust the
vuylstekeara lip veiner with cornflour
and vein the lip. Alternatively, vein
with the stargazer (B) veiner. Frill the
edges of the lip strongly, use the
needle frilling tool to accentuate the
fluting. Pinch the lip from the back to
create a central vein.

3 If you don't have the vuylstekeara
veiner, cut out a shape with the ivy

varigator cutter and cut off the broad
end. Work the edge of this shape
with a dresden tool. Moisten the
worked shape and attach it onto the
lip with the sharp end pointing down
the lip. Use a pair of curved tweezers
to pinch in the pollen guide and snip
raised pieces at the front of the callus.
Set aside to dry. Before the petal is
completely dry, dust the callus with
the deep magenta and a little deep
purple dust. The pollen guides should

be flushed with egg yellow. There should be a pale line around the callus. Carefully dust another flush of colour outwards and down the lip, leaving a pale rim around the callus. Set aside to dry, then steam to set.

Lateral petals
4 Roll out white paste, moisten a 28-gauge wire and lay it about two-thirds the length of the petal cutter length. Fold back the paste,

Dorsal sepal
5 Roll out a piece of white paste over a groove. Moisten a quarter length 28-gauge wire and place along the groove, fold back and sandwich the paste, rolling it out again. Cut out a sepal shape. The dorsal petal, if veined with a vuylstekeara veiner, will be seen to have two grooves which meet about 6mm (¼in) from the tip of the petal. If you do not have the correct veiner, this may be added

Buds
7 Roll different sizes of balls into carrot shapes, insert moistened 26- and 24-gauge wires and mark them using a 3-wire cage. Remove from the cage, curve the bud gently and then dust with a little magenta dust. Set aside to dry before steaming.

Assembly
8 Tape the column onto the lip, ensuring they are tightly fastened

sandwiching the wire, roll out the paste again and cut out the shape. Vein the petal in the stargazer (B) veiner, with the grooved side uppermost. Pinch a ridge across the petal top and then frill the sides of the petals from a little more than half the length of the petal, leaving an area close to the column unfrilled. Angle the frilling so it works with the veining of the petal. Accentuate the veining with the needle frilling tool.

with a dresden tool. The side edges of the petal curve slightly inwards, but the tip of the petal curves backwards.

Lateral sepals
6 Roll out the paste, insert a wire and cut out the petal. If you do not have a vuylstekeara veiner, vein with the stargazer (B) veiner, creating a central vein using a dresden tool. The side edges curve slightly inwards, but the sepal itself curves backwards.

together. Tape the two frilled lateral petals tightly on either side. Tape in the two lateral sepals behind and alongside the lip and finally tape in the dorsal sepal. Tape the buds in increasing sizes from the end of an 18-gauge wire; as the buds get larger increase the space in between. Add the flowers, ensuring that the petals and sepals don't get tangled. The leaves are a rich green, fairly smooth with the tips being quite curled.

Bouvardia

Bouvardia is, at present, extremely popular with florists for use in bridal arrangements. It comes in a range of soft pinks and white, and provides a wonderful, delicate background to the main flowers in a bouquet or an arrangement. For this spray, tape the buds and flowers into pairs, and then into fours. Below each set of four, add a bract made using a fuchsia sepal cutter. Steam the clusters to set the colour, then tape together, adding leaves in pairs below the bracts.

Materials
White and mid green flowerpaste

20-, 24-, 26-, 28- and 30-gauge white wires

Holly/ivy, forest green, vine green, black and lemon petal dusts

Quarter glaze

Nile green floristry tape

Cutters (TT 466, 285, 340) or page 157

Bouvardia leaf veiner

Rose petal cutters, small set (TT)

Small fuchsia sepal cutter (TT)

1 Make veiners and leaves as pages 8 and 29. Dust with holly/ivy and forest green. When dry, dip in quarter glaze.

2 For flowers, roll a small ball of white paste into a slender carrot, pinch out the top and place the flat side on the board. Roll out the paste until fairly fine. Place the fuchsia cutter over the pedestal and cut out. Elongate the petals and vein. Open the throat. Make the calyx as for the bud below. Add a little vine green and lemon into the throat. For buds, thread a bead of paste down a 30-gauge wire and work onto the wire until slender. Roll a small ball of paste, moisten the tip of the wire and insert into the ball of paste. Turn the ball into a square with a slightly domed top. Mark a line from point to point across the dome. Cut out a shape in green paste with the small daphne cutter. Thread onto the bud stem.

Tropical Scent

Vanilla, because of its climbing, trailing habit and also its extensive culinary use, is a perfect subject to display on a cake. This stunning two tier wedding cake, with its sunburst gold base stand and spiral twist flower holder, allows the vanilla orchids to twist, trail and show off their natural beauty – all that is missing is the vanilla scent! A gold lizard completes the tropical theme of this cake. *Alan*

Cake and decoration

15cm (6in) and 25cm (10in) round cakes
1.5kg (3¼lb) white almond paste
2kg (4¼lb) white sugarpaste
15cm (6in) and 25cm (10in) thin cake boards
48cm (19in) silver base stand (Fenwicks)
Broad lemon satin ribbon to trim cakes
Small amount of white flowerpaste
Edible gold dusting powder
Foliage green petal dust
Gold spray paint
Super matt spray varnish (CC)
Spiral twist candle-holder
Large separator nest (CC) and posy pick
9 vanilla orchids and 12 buds
45 vanilla orchid leaves, plus aerial roots

Preparation

1 I sprayed the originally silver base stand and the spiral twist candle-holder with the same gold spray paint. Allow to dry, then seal the gold with a matt spray varnish. Allow to dry.

2 Place both cakes onto their thin matching boards. Brush the cakes with apricot glaze and cover with white almond paste. Allow to dry. Brush the surface of the almond paste with alcohol (a vanilla flavoured liquor would be appropriate!), and then cover with white sugarpaste. Use a pair of sugarpaste smoothers to achieve a smooth neat coating. Transfer the large cake with its board to sit on top of the gold base stand.

3 Attach a band of pale lemon ribbon around the base of both cakes using either a tiny amount of royal icing or some softened sugarpaste.

Gold lizard

4 Roll out white flowerpaste and cut out the lizard design from the template on page 157. Allow to firm up a little, before painting the lizard with a mixture of edible gold dusting powder and clear alcohol. Moisten the back of the lizard with alcohol and position onto the side of the top tier. Add painted tongue, feet and eyes onto the cake. Using a mixture of foliage green petal dust and clear alcohol, add some finer detailed painting to the tongue, eyes, feet and main body. Another lizard could be added to the back of the cake.

Assembly

5 Position the perspex separator centrally on top of the base tier. Place the spiral twist candle holder over the top of the stand, then place the small cake on top of the separator with the candle holder spiralling carefully around it.

6 Wire up two trailing, yet well constructed, sprays using the vanilla orchids, buds and foliage. Insert the larger spray into the posy pick and then into the base tier. Sit the smaller spray into the tight curl at the top of the candle holder.

Vanilla orchid

Vanilla is the only orchid (*Vanilla planifolia/pompona*) grown as a commercial crop. With over a hundred species from Central America and the West Indies, only a few are grown for their beans. The Aztecs used vanilla for its perfume and culinary use. They used the seed mixed with cacao to make a drink which is the basis of chocolate today. The plants are not often grown by amateurs as they grow to about 30 metres (100 feet), and are difficult to encourage into bloom.

Materials

Creamy green and mid green flowerpaste
18-, 22-, 24-, 26- and 28-gauge white wires
Primrose, lemon, vine green, white, foliage green, forest green, edelweiss and aubergine petal dusts
Sap green craft dust
Full glaze
White and nile green floristry tape

Equipment

Vanilla orchid cutters
(TT 827–830) or templates (p 157)
Large amaryllis petal veiner (GI)
Silk veining tool (HP)
Large rose petal veiner (GI)
Plain edge cutting
wheel (PME)
Tulip leaf veiner (GI)
(optional)

Column

1 The column is quite slender in this orchid. Roll a ball of creamy green paste. Insert a moistened 22-gauge white wire into the ball and then work the paste down the wire to create a long slender column shape. Hollow out the underside of the column by pressing the length of it against the length of the rounded end of a celstick. Bend the column into a lazy 'S' shape. Pinch a backbone down the

length of the shape. Add a tiny ball of paste to the tip of the column and split down the centre with a sharp scalpel to represent the anther cap. Allow to dry overnight.

Labellum (lip/throat)

2 For the labellum, roll out some creamy green flowerpaste, leaving a slightly thicker area at the centre. Cut out the petal shape using the throat cutter or template on page 157. Vein

against the pad, and draw down a central vein using the fine end of the dresden tool. Turn the petal over and then, using a medium sized ball tool, carefully hollow out either side of the ridge. Moisten the 'V' shaped base of the petal and carefully position the column centrally (hollowed side down) against the petal. Attach the two side edges onto the column, leaving the backbone of the shape still clearly visible. Curl back the edges of

dust into the throat and at the base. Some orchids have a red tinge at the centre of the throat too – this addition is optional.

Lateral petals

4 Roll out some more paste, leaving a thick ridge for the wire – a grooved board may be used for this. Cut out the wing petal shape using either the cutter or the template and a sharp scalpel. Insert a moistened 26-gauge

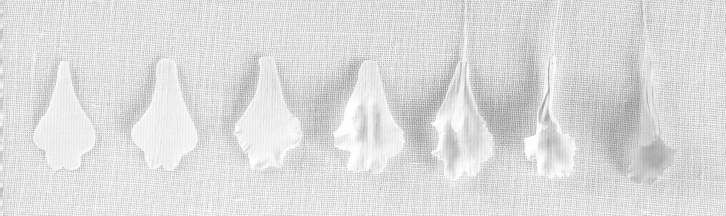

the petal using the double-sided amaryllis petal veiner. Place the petal back onto the board and, using the broad end of a dresden tool, double frill the edge of the petal by pressing and dragging the tool slightly on the edge of the paste against the board. Next, soften the frill slightly by resting the petal on the side of your index finger and work the edge at intervals with the silk veining tool. Place the petal onto a pad, right side down

the petal. Allow the labellum to firm up completely before colouring with petal dusts.

Colouring

3 The colour of the labellum varies between varieties – planifolia and pompona both have yellow lips. Mix together primrose and lemon petal dusts. Dust the labellum from the edges towards the centre using a flat brush. Add some vine green petal

wire into about a third to half the length of the petal. Soften the edge of the petal and vein using the large rose petal veiner – you will need to press firmly. Pinch the petal from the base to the tip. Repeat to make the two lateral petals. Allow to firm up either fairly straight (for a just opened flower) or curled back as a mature bloom. The flowers only bloom for a day – although the flowering season can last for some time.

Dorsal and lateral sepals

5 Repeat the instructions as in step 4, using the relevant cutters for each sepal. The sepals can be dried straight or curly as for lateral petals.

Colouring and assembly

6 Dust the petals and sepals from the base and then from the edges with a light dusting of vine green. You might prefer to add some white petal dust to the mixture.

7 Tape the two wing petals onto either side of the throat petal, and then tape in the three outer sepals using half width tape. If the petals are still pliable, reshape them to form a more realistic shaped flower.

Ovary

8 Add a sausage of pale green paste behind the orchid. Thin it between your fingers and thumb. Curve the back slightly. Using the plain edge

wheel, add a couple of veins. Dust lightly with vine and foliage green.

Buds

9 Roll a ball of creamy green paste into a cone shape. Insert a hooked, moistened 24-gauge white wire into the broad base of the cone. Work the base down onto the wire to create both the bud and ovary shape together. The tip of the bud should be quite round. Divide into three

sections using a sharp scalpel or the plain cutting wheel. Create a series of finer lines on each sepal again using a scalpel or the cutting wheel. Bend the neck of the bud gracefully. Dust as for the outer petals of the flower. Tape the buds into tight clusters.

Leaves

10 The leaves are very thick as with most orchids; however, I have made them finer for use on cakes. Roll out

mid green paste onto a grooved board. Cut out a leaf shape. Insert a moistened 26- or 24-gauge wire, depending upon the leaf size, into the thick ridge. Place the leaf onto a pad and soften the edges. Place the leaf into the tulip leaf veiner or vein using a packet of fine wire curved to the shape of the leaf and pressed onto the surface. Pinch from the base to the tip of the leaf. Make the leaves in various sizes. Allow to firm a little

before dusting. Dust with forest green, vine green and sap green craft dust. Allow to dry, then dip into a full glaze for a high gloss.

Aerial roots

11 These grow out of the leaf axils. Tape over a short length of 28-gauge wire with half width white tape. Tape over a few times but each time start lower from the tip for a tapered effect. Dust the tips with vine green.

Pods

12 These can be huge so I have scaled them down to use in arrangements and on cakes. Roll a long sausage of pale green flowerpaste. Insert a hooked 24- or 22-gauge wire (depending upon the length). Pinch the paste firmly around the wire. Smooth the pod between your palms. Create a central vein using the plain edge cutting wheel down the length of the pod. Curve

the shape slightly. Allow to firm up before dusting. Some vanilla plants produce very straight pods, others very curved banana like pods. Dust lightly with forest green. Overdust with a mixture of edelweiss and foliage green. Tinge the base and the tip with aubergine. Tape into clusters.

13 Tape an aerial root onto the end of an 18-gauge wire with half width tape. Work down the stem, adding leaves alternately. Thicken the stem with full width tape and more 18-gauge wire as the plant has fleshy stems. Introduce bud clusters, adding a leaf where they join the main stem. Form a trailing spray, adding flowers and buds. Separate stems can be used, adding pods. Dust the main stem using the colours of the leaves.

Zygopetalum Plants

This interesting orchid, *Zygopetalum intermedium* (below left), comes from Bolivia, Brazil and Peru. Among the books I was looking at for reference, I found there was another orchid in the genus which has much more delicate colouring – *Zygopetalum* 'Helen Ku' (below right). For the 'Helen Ku' variety, the sepals and petals are not marked but are a very delicate pale colour (vine green with a delicate overdusting of holly/ivy) and the lip has very pale markings. The construction is the same, only the shape of the lip and the colouring differs. *Tombi*

Zygopetalum orchid

This South American orchid (*Zygopetalum intermedium*) comes in a variety of colours. For a rich purple lip, use deep purple and African violet petal dusts, and magenta and ultramarine craft dusts.

Materials

Pale green and white flowerpaste

18-, 20-, 22-, 24-, 26-, 28- and 30-gauge white wires

Vine green, holly/ivy, jade, black, white, lemon, edelweiss, autumn green and mother of pearl petal dusts

Deep magenta craft dust

Holly berry liquid colour

Full and half glaze

Nile green floristry tape

Florists' staysoft

Equipment

Plain edge cutting wheel (PME)

Zygopetalum cutter set (TT 733, 18, 15) or templates (p 155)

Stargazer (B) veiner (GI)

Fine paintbrush for detail

Wide amaryllis veiner (GI)

Silk veining tool (HP)

Needle frilling tool (CC)

Cardboard apple trays

Zygopetalum leaf veiners made from silicone plastique, p 8 (CS)

Buds

1 Take a small ball of pale green paste and roll into a narrow teardrop. Hook a quarter length 28-gauge wire (the larger buds can be on 26-gauge), moisten and insert into the base of the bud. Work the end on securely. Mark three lines onto the bud using either a cage or a cutting wheel. Curve the tip of the bud into a curve. Allow to dry to leather hard stage. Dust the base of the bud with a little vine green and holly/ivy dust, and then the raised sections with a little deep magenta. Overdust with a jade, black and white mixture. Allow to dry completely before steaming.

Bracts

2 The bracts need to be in increasing sizes for both buds and flowers. Take a piece of very pale green paste and follow instructions for leaves on page 29. Vein with the

4 Next, pinch a U shaped ridge onto the upper surface of the column, facing backwards.

5 When the column is leather hard, dust it from the wire end with a little holly/ivy and a light dusting of deep magenta. Overdust very lightly with the jade/white/black mixture. Paint some fine vertical lines using the holly berry liquid colour underneath the column. Add some fine dots onto the

place along the groove. Fold back the paste and roll out again. Cut out the sepal using cutter No. 15. Place onto the foam pad and soften the edge with a metal ball tool. To make the dorsal sepal also elongate the shape slightly. Dust the stargazer veiner and vein the sepal. Place on the palm of your hand and, using a metal ball tool, gently cup the sepal. Pinch the tip to a sharp point and place on dimpled foam to dry.

stargazer (B) veiner and trim the base of the sepal. Place on dimpled foam to dry. Dust with a pale mixture of white, vine green and a little black.

Column

3 Make a column from very pale green paste. Insert a moistened 24-gauge wire through a carrot shape. Hollow and curve the column with a small ball tool and pinch a point on the lip.

anther cap in the depression behind the U shaped ridge. Roll a tiny piece of white paste into a ball, moisten the underside of the pointed lip and attach. Divide the ball into two. Allow to dry before steaming.

Dorsal and lateral sepals

6 For each one, repeat the same process. Roll out pale green paste over a small groove, moisten a quarter length 28-gauge wire and

7 When leather hard, dust the sepals with a little vine green at the base, and a light dusting of holly/ivy from the tip downwards. Use the holly berry liquid colour (with a little black dust added) and a fine brush to paint the typical blotches on the sepals. Overdust with the jade/white/black colour. Dry before steaming. The lateral petals are made in the same way as the sepals but using the No. 18 cutter.

Labellum (lip/throat)

8 Roll out white paste over a medium groove. Leave the paste at the edge of the board very thick. Leave the paste at the opposite end very thick as well. Moisten a 26-gauge wire and place along the groove – about 2.5cm (1in) wire in the groove. Fold back the paste and position the thick pad of paste over the wire at the edge of the board. Roll out the paste from the thick pad, leaving a

thick U shaped piece of paste. Position the cutter with the narrow end at the board edge. (The U shape should echo the width of the column and the U shape on the anther cap should mirror that on the lip.) Cut a V shape into the broad end of the petal opposite the U.

9 Dust the amaryllis veiner and vein the petal without squashing the U shape. Lift the cut out petal and

carefully broaden the petal at the wire, using a little of the thick pad of paste. You need to have a sharp 'cliff edge' at the front of the U shaped piece of paste with a slight recess behind it. Make two indentations on the underside of the thick pad of paste. Pinch two honey guides below the 'cliff face'. Use the cutting wheel to mark a series of ridges onto the thick pad of paste going up and over the U shaped ridge. Using the silk veining tool, broaden and frill the edge of the labellum, then use a frilling needle. Dry in an apple tray.

10 Use a fine brush and the holly berry liquid colour to paint broken lines on the lip, leaving about 5–8mm (¼–⅓in) white paste immediately below the padded U shape. Dust deep magenta over the heavy U shaped pad on the labellum. Leave about 5mm (¼in) of white paste

immediately below the U shape. Carefully dust a line of deep magenta where the spotty stripes start (do this lightly, fading the colour as it goes down the labellum towards the edge). Dust a little lemon petal dust at the wire end.

Pseudobulbs

11 Make pseudobulbs in two or three sizes, following the instructions on page 142.

Leaves

12 Make leaves in different sizes, ensuring they are in pairs, following the instructions on page 142.

13 Make a few 'special' leaves. Insert a 26-gauge wire into a leaf (it should be quite a short distance up the wire) and then spiral the leaf. These spiralled leaves are from where the flower spikes emerge and are a darker green than the leaves just below it, deepening once again to the lowest, most mature leaves. I prefer not to make these leaves until I have the flower spikes assembled and then I encase the flower spike in the leaf, leaving sufficient wire to be pushed into the staysoft to keep it firmly upright. Continue making leaves.

Assembling the flowers
14 Tape the column to the lip. Tape the two petals on either side of the column. Tape in the lateral sepals on either side of the petals. Tape in the dorsal sepal. Tape down the stem for 1cm (½in) before taping in a bract.

Assembling the flower spikes
15 Tape the stem of each bud with green tape, adding bracts to each one. Tape 3–5 buds and bracts onto an 18-gauge wire. Add the flowers below the buds, leaving increasing gaps as they get larger.

Assembling the plant
16 Tape two large leaves together (centre veins facing towards the centre). Trim off the wire and moisten. Push firmly into the pseudo-bulb. Take a small piece of pale green paste and work it from the base of the leaves to the top of the neck of the pseudobulb. Make a neat collar. Dust with autumn leaf mixed with a little white. Repeat this process using small leaves on the small pseudobulb and medium leaves on the medium pseudobulb. Arrange the leaves in pairs below and opposite one another, curving around the base of the pseudobulbs. The leaves curve around to encase the base of the pseudobulb, with the tips curving away slightly. The leaves are layered one upon the other. There are between two and five layers of leaves below each pseudobulb. It easier to tape them together when they are still soft enough to bend slightly. Dry completely before inserting into the staysoft. The flower spikes emerge from one of the curled leaves. They are then bracketed by medium leaves, then larger leaves and then each pair once again decreases in size until the final layer of leaves are almost as small as the larger bracts. These are at ground level. Fill the pot with staysoft and add a sprinkling of 'coconut bark'. Push the bulb wires into the staysoft, clustering them together. Use a pair of strong pliers to bend the wire below the leaves on the flower spike. These emerge from immediately alongside a large bulb.

Aerial roots
17 Roll long pieces of very pale green paste onto 26-gauge wires. Overdust with white dust and white or mother of pearl bridal satin. Arrange them at the edge of the pot.

Miltassia Magic

This beautiful design would make an interesting alternative, contemporary Christmas cake. A stunning display of rich red *Miltassia* orchids and pink gaura flowers has been given a seasonal touch with the addition of decorative sugar frosted wire to each spray. *Tony*

Cake and decoration

25cm (10in) elliptical cake

800g (1¾lb) white almond paste

1kg (2¼lb) shell pink sugarpaste

30cm (12in) elliptical cake board

3mm pink ribbon to trim cake

15mm pink ribbon to trim board

Spruce green, claret and chestnut brown paste colours

White petal dust

4 stems of frosted red wires (step 8)

Flowers

4 miltassia orchids and buds

3 stems of gaura

5 hydrangea leaves (p 46)

Equipment

Small and large posy picks

Preparation

1 Brush the cake with apricot glaze and cover with almond paste. Leave to dry. Moisten the surface of the almond paste with clear alcohol and cover with sugarpaste using smoothers to achieve a good finish.

2 Cover the cake board with sugarpaste and position the cake on top, making sure it is central and that there is a neat join between the cake base and board.

3 Attach a band of thin pink ribbon to the base of the cake using a tiny amount of royal icing.

4 Place double-sided tape around the edge of the board and secure a band of pink ribbon to the edge of the board.

5 Either paint the design freehand, or use the template on page 152. Use the spruce green paste colour and the white petal dust diluted with a small amount of isopropyl alcohol to paint the stem and leaves of the gaura.

6 Using a little claret paste colour and the white petal dust diluted with a small amount of isopropyl alcohol to make a pale pink colour, paint the gaura flowers onto the cake. Add the stamens using diluted chestnut brown paste colour.

Assembly

7 The red frosted wires give the cake a slight sparkle and, set against the red miltassia orchids, add warmth to the cake.

8 Dip the cut red wires into fresh egg white and then into caster sugar. Leave to dry.

9 First, wire up the main spray by taping three miltassia orchids together at various heights, adding four buds and the three stems of gaura. Finally, add the stems of wires and three hydrangea leaves.

10 For the small spray, tape together one orchid and a bud, then a stem of wires and finally add two hydrangea leaves.

11 Insert both sprays into the posy picks and insert into the cake, leaving the top of the picks showing so they can be seen when the cake is cut.

Miltassia orchid

Miltonia brassia has been especially productive in giving very warm tolerant progeny with an array of colours and forms. Hybrids with *Brassia* attain levels of perfection that would have been only dreams even twenty years ago. The flowers resemble enormous spiders on stems exceeding 40cm (16in) in height; they look spectacular on gracefully arching stems. This is one of my favourite orchids in this book.

Materials
Pale melon, ruby,
pale and mid-green flowerpaste
20-, 24-, 26- and 28-gauge white wires
White, primrose, ruby, moss green,
aubergine and foliage green petal dusts
Nile green floristry tape
Half glaze

Equipment
Miltassia orchid cutters (TT 878–880) or
templates (p 152)
Miltonia lip veiner made from silicone
plastique, p8 (CS)
Stargazer (B) veiner (GI)
Plain edge cutting wheel (PME)
Long leaf orchid veiner made from silicone
plastique, p8 (CS)

Column
1 Roll a small ball of pale melon
flowerpaste into a cigar shape to form
the column. Insert a small, moistened,
hooked 24-gauge white wire into the
upper half of the column.

2 Press the flatter end of a dresden
tool into the column, easing the paste
out to the either side of the column.
Place the column on a board and flute
either side using a dresden tool, then

form a small anther cap to the tip of the column.

Labellum (lip/throat)

3 Roll out out a piece of ruby flowerpaste, leaving a ridge in the centre of the paste. Cut out the lip using the lip cutter or the template on page 152 and insert a small hooked 26-gauge white wire. Roll a very small ball of flowerpaste and press it into the dip in the top half of the veiner to form the raised platform. Soften the edges of the lip petal and place in the veiner to vein. Remove from veiner and place edge of the lip on your finger and, using a cocktail stick, roll the edge of the petal in the same direction as the veins in the petal. Place the lip on dimpled foam and leave to dry.

Sepals and petals

4 Roll out ruby flowerpaste, leaving a ridge in the centre of the paste. Cut out two lateral petals and one dorsal sepal using the longer of the petal cutters. Moisten a 28-gauge wire and insert into the thicker end of the petals. Soften the edges and vein using the stargazer (B) veiner. Pinch a centre vein into the two lateral sepals, then place on foam to dry.

5 Roll and cut out two petals using the smaller petal cutters, then moisten a 28-gauge wire and insert into the thicker end of the petals. Soften the edges, then vein using the stargazer (B) veiner. Pinch a centre vein in each petal and form a nice point on each petal. Place on dimpled foam to dry.

Colouring
6 Dust the column by mixing a little white petal dust with primrose, then dust the tip of the anther cap and the

between the strokes with a few spots of ruby.

8 Dust the sepals and petals with ruby petal dust. Randomly paint small semi circles of white petal dust mixed with clear alcohol on each of the petals and sepals.

Assembly
9 Tape the column to the lip using nile green floristry tape. Add the two

11 Moisten the inside of each petal and place onto the cone, overlapping the petals slightly and bending them back at the tip. Dust the buds with moss green petal dust and the edges with ruby mixed with a little aubergine petal dust.

Leaves and pseudobulbs
12 Roll a long length of mid green paste, leaving a ridge down the centre. Cut out a long leaf, insert a

inside of the column, and the sides and top with ruby petal dust. Dust the edges of the lip with ruby petal dust, drawing the brush up the petal to the raised platform.

7 Paint the top of the raised platform by mixing primrose petal dust with a little alcohol and paint fine strokes of primrose from the raised platform down the lip for approximately 1cm (½in), filling in

arm petals and then the head sepal and finally two leg sepals.

Buds
10 Roll a small ball of pale green paste onto a hooked 20-gauge white wire, tapering the paste to a long cone. Roll out pale green paste and cut out two petals using the smaller petal cutter. Vein and pinch a centre vein down the centre of each petal, cupping the base with a ball tool.

moistened 24-gauge wire into the thick ridge and vein using the veiner. Pinch the leaf from the base up the central vein. Allow to dry. Dust with moss and foliage. Dip in half glaze.

13 Roll a ball of mid green paste, flattening slightly. Insert the leaf wire into the top, working the paste to a long oval. Vein the sides. Tape a single stem of flowers to the bulb side, adding a further leaf to either side.

Silver birch

A few species of birch are low growing shrubs, but most are trees with a graceful habit, with wonderful whitish or grey papery bark. Silver birch (*Betula pendula*) is a native to both Europe and Asia. The foliage is small with a pretty serrated edge that makes it an interesting addition to both arrangements and sprays.

Materials
Pale holly/ivy flowerpaste
20- and 28-gauge white wires
Forest green, primrose, moss green and champagne petal dusts
Isopropyl alcohol
Quarter glaze
Brown floristry tape

Equipment
Silver birch templates (p 152)
Birch leaf veiner from silicone plastique, p 8 (CS) or birch/hazel veiner (GI)

1 Roll out pale holly/ivy paste quite thinly, leaving a thick ridge for the wire. Cut out the leaf shape. Insert a moistened 28-gauge white wire into half the thick ridge. For the serrated edge, use a sharp scalpel at intervals to flick away part of the edge of the leaf. Soften the edge using a ball tool. Place the leaf into a homemade birch leaf veiner or a birch/hazel veiner. Squeeze well. Remove and pinch it from the base to the tip.

2 Dust with forest green from the base, fading out to the edges. Overdust with primrose, then moss green. Paint a central vein using champagne mixed with alcohol. When dry, dip into a quarter glaze or steam.

3 Create a leaf bud at the end of a 20-gauge wire using half width tape. Keep taping in one place to build bulk, then tape up to the tip and down. Add foliage in pairs down the twig.

Gaura

Gaura lindheimeri is a native to the warmer parts of North America. It produces long graceful stems with very delicate butterfly shaped flowers which can be pure white, pale or a rosy pink. Although they are often planted in herbaceous borders in Britain, they are not reliably hardy in harsh winters. They have a long flowering season from the spring through to early autumn, making them an ideal filler flower to mix with many different seasonal flowers.

Materials

Fine white stamens
Non-toxic hi-tack glue
20-, 24-, 28- and 30-gauge white wires
Plum, vine green, primrose, white, burgundy, moss green and foliage green petal dusts
White or pale pink and mid holly/ivy flowerpaste
Nile green floristry tape

Equipment

Gaura petal cutters (TT 868, 869) or templates (p. 152)
Christmas rose veiner (GI)
Gaura leaf cutter (TT 870–872)
Gaura leaf veiner made from silicone plastique, p8 (CS), or small gardenia leaf veiner (GI)

Stamens

1 Bunch together eight fine white stamens and one extra single stamen with its head cut off – this is for the pistil and should be slightly longer than the stamens. Using a little hi-tack glue, bond the base of the stamens together neatly, flattening them slightly. Firm up for a few minutes. Attach the stamens and pistil to a 24-gauge white wire using the glue. Allow to dry and then bend the stamens

down at a harsh angle. Curl the pistil and the tips of the stamens slightly. Dust the stamens from the base with plum petal dust, fading to white towards the tips. Dust the tips with a mixture of vine green and primrose.

Petals

2 Roll out white or pale pink paste thinly, leaving a thick area at the base for the wire. Cut out a petal shape using the gaura petal cutter. Insert a

on the edges with a pale mixture of plum and white. Some varieties have much stronger colouring at the base fading towards the petal edges. Tape the four petals onto the stamens.

Calyx

4 Roll out green paste thinly and cut out two narrow strips of paste. Divide each strip for the sepals of the calyx. Vein the centre of each sepal and pinch into a sharp point. Attach

tightly to the stem. Allow to dry. Dust lightly with primrose and vine green. Make some larger buds and insert a 28-gauge wire into the base. Divide the surface into two. Dust with plum and burgundy at the base. Dust the tip lightly with vine green petal dust.

6 Cut a single fine strip of green paste and attach onto the base of the bud. Make several wired buds and then tape onto the stem.

short length of moistened 30-gauge white wire into the thick base of the petal. Pinch the paste onto the wire to secure. Soften the edges. Place the petal into the double-sided Christmas rose veiner and press firmly. Remove and then hollow out the length of the petal using a ball tool. Repeat to make four petals.

Colouring and assembly

3 This flower has been dusted lightly

both sets onto the back of the flower and curl them back. Dust the sepal tips with plum and the rest with vine. Lightly dust the stem with burgundy mixed with plum petal dust on one side of the stem.

Buds

5 Form a small ball of paste into a slim teardrop shape and attach to the end of a 20-gauge wire. Repeat to make lots of buds and attach them

Leaves and assembly

7 Roll out mid green paste, leaving a thick ridge. Cut out the leaf. Insert a moistened 30- or 28-gauge wire into the ridge. Soften the edge. Vein using either veiner. Dust with moss and foliage. Dry, then steam to set.

8 Add wired buds to the stem, then flowers. Add the leaves alternately down the stem. Bend into a curve. Dust plum/burgundy down the stem.

Orchid Fever

A lively arrangement of South American rain forest orchids form the main feature on this long lozenge shaped cake that would be suitable for the centrepiece at a birthday celebration party. The dainty trailing stems of *Epidendrum* orchids enhance the shape of the cake beautifully, while the *Aspasia lunata* plants form the focal point of the design. *Alan*

Cake and decoration

1.75kg (4lb) pale vine green sugarpaste
25cm (10in) long lozenge cake
1.25kg (2½lb) white almond paste
36cm (14in) long cake board
Fine and broad 'lime juice' satin ribbon to trim cake and board
Vine, foliage, plum and white petal dusts
Small amount of dried tillandsia moss

Flowers

7 trailing stems of epidendrum orchids
7 aspasia orchids with foliage and pseudobulbs, plus extra foliage and bulbs

Equipment

Fine paintbrushes
Florists' staysoft
Thin piece of plastic or perspex

Preparation

1 Knead a little vine green paste colour into the sugarpaste. Brush the cake with warmed apricot glaze and then cover with white almond paste. Allow to dry. Moisten the surface of the almond paste with clear alcohol and cover with pale green sugarpaste. Use a pair of sugarpaste smoothers to achieve a neat finish. A pad of sugarpaste flattened into the palm will also help to achieve a polished finish.

2 Cover the cake board with pale green sugarpaste, trim off the edge and then smooth as for the cake. Transfer the cake slightly offset onto the board (this is to allow a larger arrangement of flowers at one side of the cake). Allow to dry.

3 Attach a fine band of lime juice ribbon around the base of the cake using a small amount of sugarpaste softened with alcohol. Glue a band of broader lime ribbon to the edge of the cake board using a glue stick.

Side design

4 Paint a freehand design onto the cake using a fine paintbrush in variations of vine green, foliage green and plum petal dust mixed and then diluted with clear alcohol. The design is a series of curls made up from dots, squares and triangular shapes. Some of the shapes should curl up onto the upper surface of the cake too.

Assembly

5 The flowers in the large arrangement have been arranged into staysoft. This should not touch the cake surface – so I have glued the staysoft onto a thin piece of plastic (from the art shop) cut to fit the side of the cake. Allow the glue to bond the two mediums together and then arrange the flowers into it. This can be done on or off the cake. Use the epidendrums to trail and twist to form the main structure of the arrangement. Next, create the focal point with the aspasia orchids, foliage and pseudobulbs. Add extra leaves to hide the excess staysoft or cover with a thin layer of florists' tillandsia moss. The smaller group of flowers have been taped together and simply rested against the cake and board.

Aspasia orchid

Aspasia lunata belongs to a small genus of about only ten species. They originate from the tropical Americas and, although not very common in cultivation, are very easy houseplants. The pretty star shaped flowers appear from the base of each pseudobulb. Due to the plant's naturally epiphytic nature, this orchid has a creeping habit.

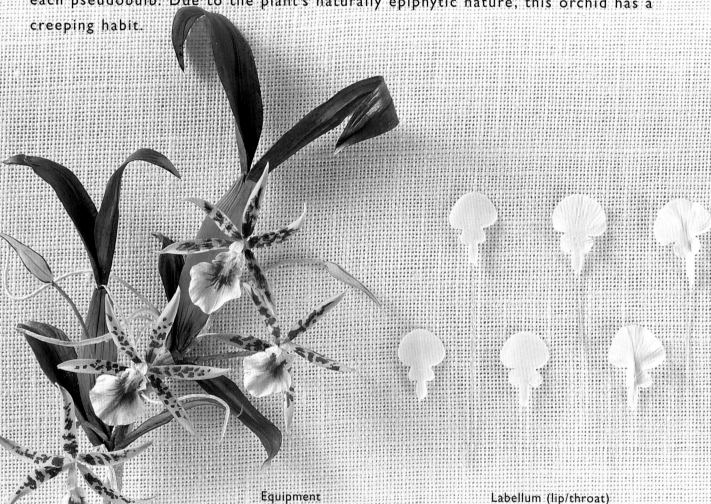

Materials
White, pale and mid green flowerpaste
20-, 22-, 24-, 26-, 28- and 30-gauge white wires
Deep magenta craft dust
Vine green, edelweiss, foliage green, aubergine and forest green petal dusts
Isopropyl alcohol
Half glaze
Nile green and white floristry tape

Equipment
Nasturtium petal cutter (TT 446)
Silk veining tool (HP)
Small tiger lily cutter (TT 426)
Plain edge cutting wheel (PME)
or sharp scalpel
Tulip leaf veiner (GI)

Labellum (lip/throat)
1 Roll out white paste thinly, leaving a thick ridge to insert a fine wire. Cut out the petal shape using the nasturtium cutter. Insert a moistened 28-gauge white wire into the thick ridge, holding the paste firmly between your finger and thumb to prevent the wire piercing through.

2 Thin out and flatten the narrow base section of the petal against the wire. Trim off any excess paste. Next, vein the surface of the petal using the veining tool; I usually rest the petal on the side of my index finger and then work the silk veining tool on each section of the petal to create fan shaped veins. Increase the pressure on the very edges to frill slightly. Pinch the petal down the centre to create a central vein. Bend the petal down slightly from the base section to create a flatter face to the flower.

Outer petals/sepals

4 First, squeeze the tiger lily cutter to produce a narrower petal shape. Roll out either white or very pale green paste thinly, leaving a thick ridge at the centre for the wire. Cut out the petal shape using the modified cutter. Insert a moistened 30-gauge white wire into the thick ridge. Soften the edges of the petal very gently – do not try to frill. Pinch the petal from the base to the tip to

creating a flared colouring. Add extra detail lines (if desired) by diluting craft dust with alcohol and painting them carefully over the magenta dusted area. As the flowers mature the lip colour fades to a much paler bluish pink. Dust the back of the column very lightly with vine green mixed with edelweiss, keeping the very tip of the column white. Add a painted white patch over the deep magenta just below the column.

Column

3 To make the column, form a small ball of white flowerpaste into a teardrop shape. Hollow out the underside of the teardrop slightly using the rounded end of the silk veining tool. Moisten the underside of the column and attach onto the base section of the petal. Carefully lift up the 'face' of the column slightly, so that it casts a gentle shadow onto the labellum.

create a central vein and a slight ridge on the back of the petal. Repeat this process to make five petals. The petals are quite flat with a gentle curve at the tip.

Colouring

5 It is always easier to dust the petals before they have had a chance to dry as you can achieve stronger colouring. Dust a patch of deep magenta craft dust onto the lip,

6 Dust the outer petals lightly with vine green. Overdust with edelweiss. Add some painted spots or blotches to the upper surface of each petal using a mixture of aubergine petal dust and alcohol. The back of each petal has a fine green line painted with diluted foliage green.

Assembly

7 Using half width white floristry tape, tape two of the petals onto either side of the lip. Next, add the remaining three petals to represent the dorsal and lateral sepals. If the petals are still pliable, you will be able to re-adjust them to create a more natural finish. Curve the stem slightly. Dust very lightly with vine green.

Buds

8 Form a ball of paste into a slender teardrop shape. Insert a moistened 26-gauge wire into the broad end.

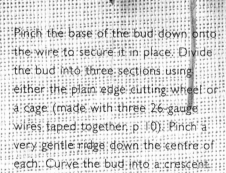

Pinch the base of the bud down onto the wire to secure it in place. Divide the bud into three sections using either the plain edge cutting wheel or a cage (made with three 26-gauge wires taped together, p.10). Pinch a very gentle ridge down the centre of each. Curve the bud into a crescent.

9 Dust lightly with vine green and an overdusting of edelweiss. Paint a fine green line over each of the three

ridges on the bud. Tape over the wire with white tape. Dust with vine dust.

Leaves

10 Roll out a length of mid green paste, leaving a thick ridge for the wire. Cut out a strap-like leaf shape. Insert a moistened 24- or 22-gauge wire into the thick ridge of the leaf. Vein using the double-sided tulip leaf veiner. Pinch the leaf from the base to the tip. Allow to firm up over a gentle curve. The leaves usually grow in pairs and one is generally slightly smaller than the other.

Colouring

11 Dust the leaves with forest, foliage and vine green petal dusts. Allow to dry. Dip into a half glaze.

Aerial roots

12 Tape over several lengths of 28-gauge wire with half width white tape.

Add extra layers at the base of each to thicken slightly. Dust the tips very lightly with vine green and edelweiss.

Assembly and pseudobulbs

13 Tape two leaves onto a 20-gauge wire. Roll a ball of green paste and thread it onto the base of the leaves. Work the paste down the wire to form an elliptical shape. Flatten the shapes. Pinch a slight ridge down either side. Vein the surface of the bulb using a fine scalpel or cutting wheel. Dust the pseudobulb with vine green and foliage. Dust around the base of the leaves with aubergine. Allow to dry. Glaze as for the leaves.

14 Tape a single or several flowers and buds at the base of each bulb. Add a couple of smaller leaves and aerial roots at the base.

Epidendrum radicans

Epidendrum radicans, from tropical America, is orange and yellow, but there are many cultivated varieties with flowers in shades of red, pink, mauve, yellow and white. They are commonly known as the crucifix orchid because of the cross shape of the lip. *Epidendrum* orchids are very useful as fillers in sprays and bouquets because of their size and trailing stems. The flowers and buds appear in clusters.

Materials

White flowerpaste
Epidendrum orchid cutters (TT)
28- and 30-gauge white wires
Lemon and African violet petal dusts
Deep magenta craft dust
Nile green floristry tape

1 Roll out white paste thinly, leaving a thick ridge. Cut out the lip. Insert a 28-gauge wire into the ridge. Pinch the petal base around the wire,

thinning a little. Create fine hairs on the four lip sections. Use the broad end of a dresden tool to flatten the hairs a little. Pinch the lip back on itself to create an angle and slight ridge to the front. Snip three cuts to create 'two eyes' and a 'nose'. Add a fine sausage of paste onto the lip for the column. Hollow out the end.

2 For back petals, form paste into a teardrop. Pinch out the broad base to

form a pedicel and thin out. Cut out the flower using the outer five-petal cutter. Elongate each petal and soften the edges. Pinch at the tip. Open up the centre slightly, moisten and pull through the wired lip petal. Thin the back and remove excess. Dust the 'eyes' and 'nose' with lemon. Colour the flower — these are magenta and African violet. Leave the column tip white. The buds have long necks wired onto 30- or 28- gauge wires.

Tequila Sunrise

Collaborating on the writing of a book is difficult. It can only work if the authors are of like mind, and the standard of work is similar. It was felt that it was a good idea to produce one or two arrangements which would combine some of the flowers we had made for different individual projects, proving just how compatible our styles and sense of colour are. *Alan, Tony and Tombi*

Flowers

7 vanilla orchids and their foliage (p 120)
2 stems of comparettia orchids (p 90)
3 peach laeliocattleya orchids (p 58)
3 red burrageara orchids (p 98)
5 stems of sage leaves (p 29)
Several extra pieces of assorted orchid foliage

Equipment

18-gauge wire
Nile green floristry tape
Florists' staysoft
Elephant design candle holder (J Lewis)
Wire cutters
Long-nosed pliers

Preparation

1 Strengthen any of the long trailing stems and larger flowers that might need it by taping 18-gauge wire alongside the main stem using half or even sometimes full width nile green tape. Attach a large ball of staysoft onto the platform at the top of the candle holder.

Assembly

2 The three trailing stems of vanilla orchids and their foliage define the main outline and flow of the arrangement. Sometimes, a hook in the end of each flower stem helps to give them extra support.

3 Next, introduce the two stems of comparettia orchids, creating a line of colour through the arrangement. Add the three laeliocattleya orchids at the centre of the arrangement to create the focal point. Try to arrange the orchids so that they are facing in slightly different directions.

4 Create another line of colour using the red burrageara orchids. Curve the bud stems to follow the lines of the arrangement. Finally, fill in the gaps in the arrangement with the sage and orchid leaves. At this stage, you will need to use long-nosed pliers to thread the components into the arrangement without breaking them or the pieces already arranged. When all the flowers and foliage have been added, stand back and view the piece as a whole. Re-adjust as necessary.

Pink Perfection

For this lovely arrangement, choose a suitable vase, staysoft and decorative gravel. Insert the staysoft into the vase. Add 5 stems of ruscus sprays or similar foliage to create an outline, then 5 sprays of the *Lemboglossum* orchids. Finally, add 5 'Radox Bouquet' roses and 5 sprays of bouvardia (page 117). The instructions for the *Lemboglossum* are on pages 110–111. To colour this orchid, dust with lemon on the raised lip section, adding vine green. Mix deep magenta, permanent rose and edelweiss, and apply to the petals. Add a few pink spots. Mix nutkin brown and black, then paint squiggly lines across each petal and sepal. Overdust with vine and edelweiss. *Tombi*

'Radox Bouquet' rose

'Radox Bouquet' is a floribunda rose. The flowers grow in wonderfully scented clusters in the summer through to late autumn. It has a rich fragrance and mid toned glossy leaves, and had just the right colouring and shape for the arrangement I had in mind.

Materials

Very pale melon and mid green flowerpaste

18-, 26-, 28- and 30-gauge white wires

Lemon, vine green, edelweiss, holly/ivy and forest green petal dusts

Deep magenta craft dust

White bridal satin dust

Quarter glaze

Nile green floristry tape

Equipment

Rose petal cutters (TT 276, 549–551)

Very large rose petal veiner (GI)

Smooth porcelain tool (HP)

Cardboard apple tray cups

Needle frilling tool (CC)

Rose calyx cutter (R11B)

3 sizes green pointed rose leaf cutters (JL10)

Large rose leaf veiner (GI)

Cone

1 Take a piece of the very pale melon flowerpaste and roll it into a smooth ball, then into a long, pointed cone with a broad base. Moisten and insert a half length 18-gauge hooked wire. Place the cone (on the wire) on the board and roll it until you have achieved a cone with a sharp point. The cone should be at least 5mm (¼ in) shorter than the smallest petal cutter. The cones must be very dry

before attempting to add any of the rose petals.

Petals

2 Roll out some very pale melon paste – not too fine, or there will be no movement in your petals. Cut out six petals with the smallest sized cutter. Place five under a fleximat until required. Take a petal, place it on a foam pad and soften the edge with a metal ball tool. Dust the petal

3 Place the next five petals on the foam pad and soften the edges with the metal ball tool, then vein each petal in turn with the petal veiner. Moisten down the left side of the petals. Place the rose cone with the first petal to the centre of the second petal and stick the petal in place, ensuring that the petal is taller than the first petal which has been stuck to the cone. Moisten the left side of each of the other petals and stick

petals are tucked in between them. Using the next size cutter, repeat the same procedure for the next layer of petals; this time use the smooth porcelain tool to roll back the free edges of the petals slightly.

4 Graduating to the next sized cutter, repeat the process; after veining the petals, cup them by placing your thumbs in the centre of the petal and by gently but firmly

veiner with cornflour and vein the petal. Moisten the petal and place the cone on the petal. If you are making a bud, make sure the base of the cone is covered by the petal but, if you are making a full rose, concentrate only on the top edge of the petal. Roll the petal around the cone, creating a very tight spiral at the tip. (You must not be able to see the cone at all.) Prepare all the rose cones following these instructions.

them to the cone. The last petal to be attached is tucked tightly beneath the first petal that was stuck in place so all the petals are spiralled. Check that all the petals are the same height. Tighten the petals by tugging them gently up and then, with a twist of the wrist, pull the petals tight at the top so that a very tight centre is created. The first petal should just be visible. Do not stick the free edges of the petals down as the next layer of

pulling the petal sideways so the centre will cup without losing too much veining. Work the edge of the petals with the frilling needle using the side of your forefinger on which to work. Be careful not to make the edges frilly; the pressure should only be on the edge of the petal. This is most easily achieved by lifting the front of the frilling needle. The edges should be very lightly softened. Only the first petal gets tucked in: the others are then attached to the centre, overlapping them in the opposite direction so that the petals, when you reach the last one, are still spiralled. Use the smooth porcelain tool to shape the petals. Do not curl the petals back across the top of the petals, they should all be brought to an attractive point.

Wired petals
5 Use the largest petal cutter to cut

6 Vein the petals; work the edges of the petals slightly more strongly with the frilling needle and cup them well by the tugging method. Shape the edges of the petals attractively and place in the apple cups to set; at this point, make absolutely sure that you have a beautiful curve to the petal (if there is a wire inserted up the petal this should be curved as well) and wire. Allow the petals to set until leather hard.

soft pink colour. Check the colouring on a spare petal specially made for this purpose.

9 Load the brush with colour and firmly tap it onto the centre of the rose to get the colour imbedded between the central petals. Continue dusting the centre until you have a lovely, smooth wash of colour on the rose. The wired petals should be dusted from the centre outwards

out five petals. This time the paste should be thicker up the centre of the petal and at the pointed tip. Moisten quarter length 26-gauge wires and insert into the paste. This can either be done so it extends to about a third to half length of the petal, or if you prefer, make a hook at one end of the wire, moisten it and insert into the pointed tip of the petal. Ensure that the petal is tightly fastened to the wire.

Colouring and assembly
7 Start by dusting a little pale lemon onto the base of each petal (at the wire) on both the back and front. You should also add yellow down between the petals on the rose centre, being careful not to get yellow on the petal edges. Add a tiny touch of vine green to the tip of the petal (at the wire).

8 Mix up some deep magenta with the edelweiss until you have a lovely,

(leaving the green and yellow showing); the colour should be faded out to the very palest of pink (almost white) at the edges. This should be done to both the back and the front of the petals.

10 Tape the petals to the centre. First tape three around the centre, and then attach the last two by inserting them between the centre and the petals that are already taped

in place. Arrange the petals as attractively and naturally as possible, then attach the calyx.

Calyx

11 Roll green paste into a ball and then into a cone. Pinch out flat leaving a short, narrow pedicel which will fit through the hole in the cutter. Roll out the paste using a medium celstick. Put the calyx cutter over the pedicel and cut out the shape.

sepals with holly/ivy and forest green dust, being careful to leave a paler edge to the sepals.

12 Moisten the centre of the calyx and attach to the base of the rose. The sepals should be arranged over the joins between the petals. To create a natural looking rose, carefully curve the sepals down, while keeping the inward curve to them as well. Steam roses lightly to set the dust.

cutter over the wire in the groove and cut out the leaf. Soften the edge of the leaf on a foam pad with a metal ball tool and then, after dusting the leaf veiner well with cornflour, vein the leaf. Arrange the leaves attractively on dimpled foam to dry to leather hardness.

14 Dust the leaf from the wire with forest green dust, fading out as you get towards the edges, then overdust

Elongate each sepal. Place on a foam pad and soften the edges of the calyx. Use fine bladed curved scissors to cut the fine hairs on the edge of the sepals. Form a groove down the centre of each sepal by using either a dresden tool or a ball tool (this will make the sepals curl upwards). Reinforce this with the veiner end of the dresden tool. Dust the inside of the sepals with the white bridal satin. Carefully dust the centres of the

Leaves

13 Choosing the smallest groove possible, roll out mid green paste along a groove, place a moistened wire (28- or 30-gauge wire for the smallest leaves, 28- or 26-gauge for the medium and large leaves) along the pale line of paste in the groove. Roll over the wire with your rolling pin and ensure the wire is embedded in the paste. Fold back the paste over the wire and roll out again. Place the

with holly/ivy dust. If you want to link the leaf to the colour of the flower, dust a little deep magenta craft dust onto the edges of the leaf. Glaze with quarter glaze when the leaf is completely dry.

15 Tape the leaves together with one large leaf between two medium leaves. Finish off by attaching two smaller leaves on either side. Tape onto the stems of the roses.

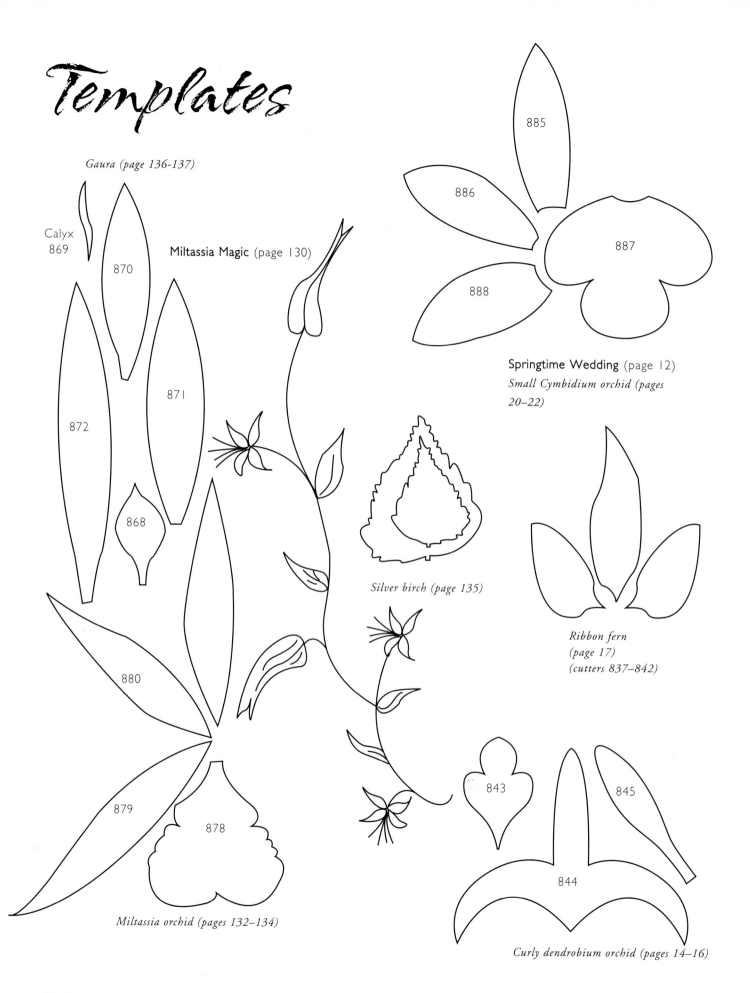

Templates

Gaura (page 136-137)

Calyx
869

870

Miltassia Magic (page 130)

871

872

868

885

886

887

888

Springtime Wedding (page 12)
Small Cymbidium orchid (pages 20–22)

Silver birch (page 135)

Ribbon fern
*(page 17)
(cutters 837–842)*

880

879

878

843

845

844

Miltassia orchid (pages 132–134)

Curly dendrobium orchid (pages 14–16)

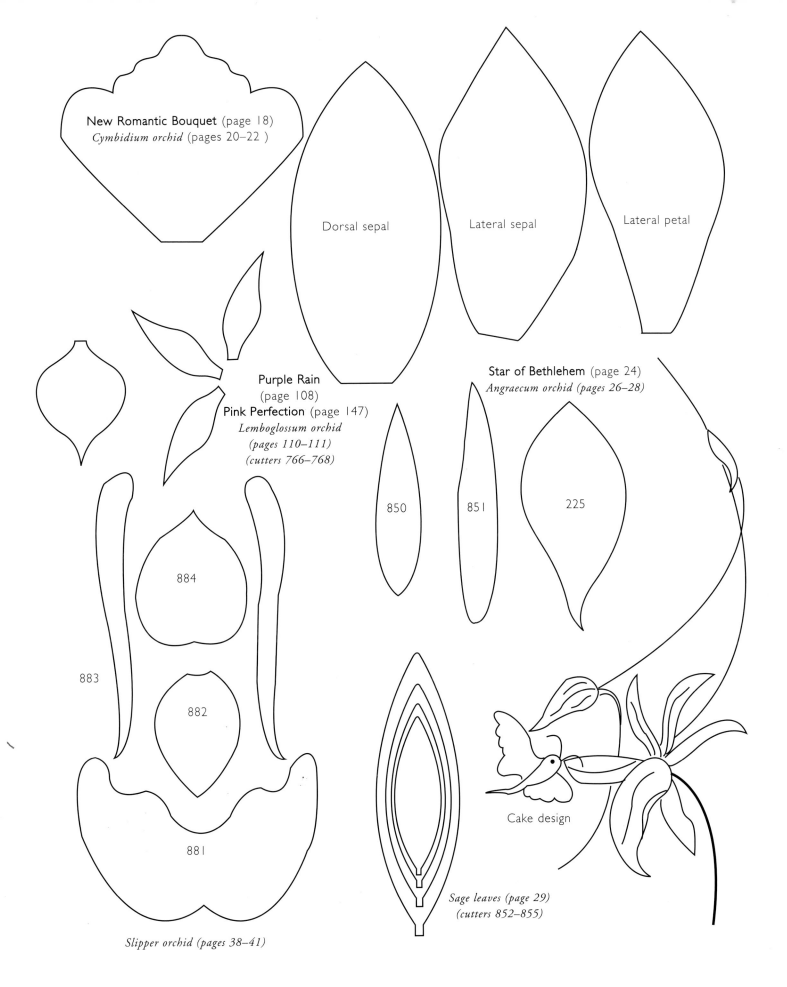

New Romantic Bouquet (page 18)
Cymbidium orchid (pages 20–22)

Dorsal sepal

Lateral sepal

Lateral petal

Purple Rain
(page 108)
Pink Perfection (page 147)
Lemboglossum orchid
(pages 110–111)
(cutters 766–768)

Star of Bethlehem (page 24)
Angraecum orchid (pages 26–28)

850

851

225

884

883

882

881

Cake design

Slipper orchid (pages 38–41)

Sage leaves (page 29)
(cutters 852–855)

Madam Butterfly (pages 30–35)
Papilionanthe orchid (pages 32–35)
(cutters 813–816)

Dorsal sepal

Lateral petal

Lateral sepal

Labellum

Column

Leaves

Oriental Delight (page 42)

Hydrangea (pages 44–46)

Bracts

Cake design

Calyx length

Bamboo orchid (pages 47–49)
(cutters 817–820)

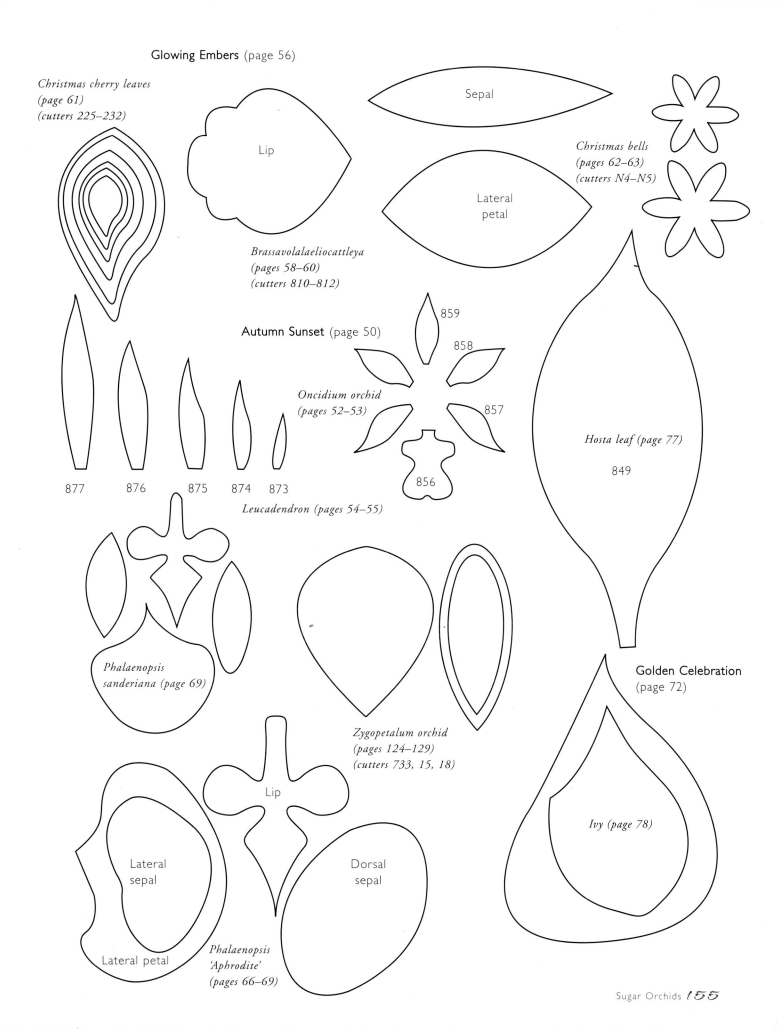

Glowing Embers (page 56)

Christmas cherry leaves
(page 61)
(cutters 225–232)

Lip

Sepal

Lateral
petal

Christmas bells
(pages 62–63)
(cutters N4–N5)

Brassavolalaeliocattleya
(pages 58–60)
(cutters 810–812)

859

858

Autumn Sunset (page 50)

Oncidium orchid
(pages 52–53)

857

Hosta leaf (page 77)

849

877   876   875   874   873

856

Leucadendron (pages 54–55)

Phalaenopsis
sanderiana (page 69)

Zygopetalum orchid
(pages 124–129)
(cutters 733, 15, 18)

Golden Celebration
(page 72)

Ivy (page 78)

Lip

Lateral
sepal

Dorsal
sepal

Lateral petal

Phalaenopsis
'Aphrodite'
(pages 66–69)

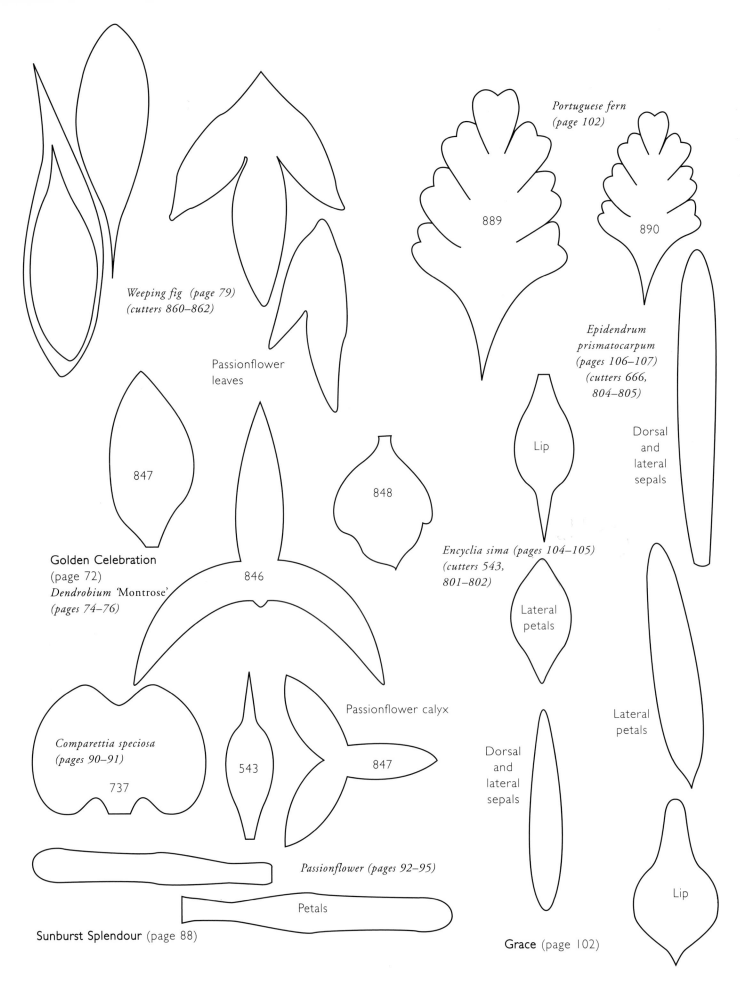

Portuguese fern
(page 102)

889

890

Weeping fig (page 79)
(cutters 860–862)

Passionflower
leaves

Epidendrum
prismatocarpum
(pages 106–107)
(cutters 666,
804–805)

847

848

Lip

Dorsal
and
lateral
sepals

Golden Celebration
(page 72)
Dendrobium 'Montrose'
(pages 74–76)

846

Encyclia sima (pages 104–105)
(cutters 543,
801–802)

Lateral
petals

Passionflower calyx

Comparettia speciosa
(pages 90–91)

737

543

847

Lateral
petals

Dorsal
and
lateral
sepals

Passionflower (pages 92–95)

Petals

Lip

Sunburst Splendour (page 88)

Grace (page 102)

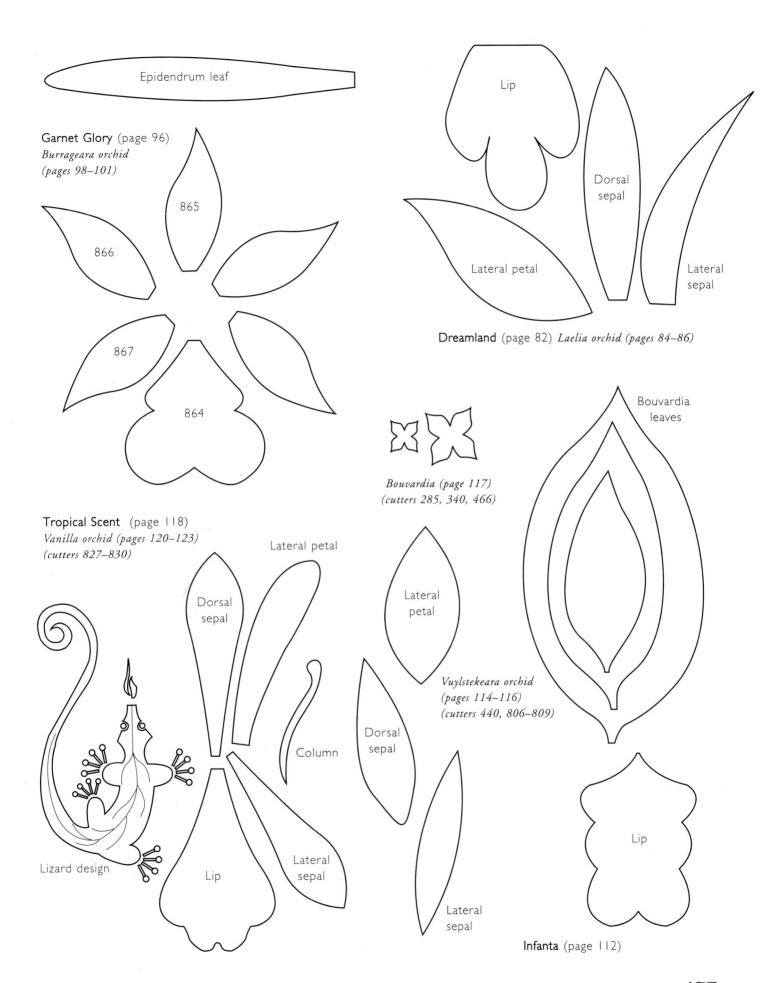

Epidendrum leaf

Garnet Glory (page 96)
*Burrageara orchid
(pages 98–101)*

865

866

867

864

Lip

Dorsal
sepal

Lateral petal

Lateral
sepal

Dreamland (page 82) *Laelia orchid (pages 84–86)*

*Bouvardia (page 117)
(cutters 285, 340, 466)*

Bouvardia
leaves

Tropical Scent (page 118)
*Vanilla orchid (pages 120–123)
(cutters 827–830)*

Dorsal
sepal

Lateral petal

Column

Lip

Lateral
sepal

Lizard design

Lateral
petal

Dorsal
sepal

Lateral
sepal

*Vuylstekeara orchid
(pages 114–116)
(cutters 440, 806–809)*

Lip

Infanta (page 112)

Dedication

Tombi Peck

I would like to dedicate my part of this book to the memory of a dear friend, Muffie MacKenzie, in gratitude; also, to my youngest granddaughter, Grace Victoria.

Alan Dunn

With love to my parents, Avril and Allen Dunn, and good friend Alice Christie.

Tony Warren

I would like to dedicate this book to my late parents, Doris and Stan Warren.

Acknowledgements

I would like to thank all the people who have helped with the production of this book, but in particular Barbara Croxford, for her never ending patience, Sue Atkinson for (as usual) her superb photography and, of course, my co-conspirators, Tony and Alan. Thanks boys! I would also like to thank Deanna de la Fuente, Yvette Angela-Duncan, John Quoi Hoi and Heather Evans for providing orchid samples, diagrams and illustrations from such distances; we couldn't have done without their help.

Thank you to everyone who played a part in the completion of this book. To our commissioning editor, Barbara Croxford – you're a star! Not an easy task trying to juggle three odd balls! To Sue Atkinson for the beautiful photography in this book, and for her own juggling skills too! Thank you also to the following for all of your help: John Quai Hoi, Landy Kober, Heather Evans, Yvette Duncan, Deana de la Fuente, Conor Day, Gill Barrowclough, Sue Burnham, Jenny Walker and Norma Laver, Beverley and Robert Dutton, Ross Nutkin, and Joan Mooney. Finally, thank you to my fellow orchid thieves – Alice, Tombi and Tony.

Thank you to my wife Alma, my two children Emily and Matthew, and my three sisters for their support while writing this book. A very big thank you goes to my boss Keith and his wife Karen for allowing me time off work; and to Angie, June and Sue for standing in for me in my absence. To all who have worked so very hard on the production of this book, especially our commissioning editor, Barbara Croxford, and to Sue Atkinson for the beautiful photographs in this book. Thank you to my Auntie Kathleen and Uncle Frank for allowing me to use their Golden Wedding cake in this book. Thank you to Tombi, Alan and Sally Harris for helping me with the text.

Suppliers

A Piece of Cake [APOC]
18 Upper High Street
Thame, Oxon, OX9 3EX
tel./fax. 0184 421 3428
sales@sugaricing.com
Distributor for Great Impressions (GI)

Cakes, Classes and Cutters
23 Princes Road
Brunton Park, Gosforth
Newcastle-upon-Tyne
NE3 5TT
tel./fax. 0191 217 0538

Celcakes and Celcrafts [CC]
Springfield House
Gate Helmsley, York, YO4 1NF
tel./fax. 01759 371 447

Confectionery Supplies [CS]
31 Lower Cathedral Road
Cardiff, Gwent, CF11 6LU
tel. 02920 372 161

Cooks Corner
50 Clayton Road
Newcastle-upon-Tyne
NE1 4PF
tel. 0191 261 5481

Country Cutters
Lower Tresauldu
Dingestow, Monmouth
Gwent, NP5 4BQ
tel. 01600 740 448

Culpitt Cake Art, Culpitt Ltd
Jubilee Industrial Estate
Ashington, Northumberland
NE63 8UQ
tel. 01670 814 545

Devon Ladye Products [DL]
Devon Ladye
The Studio, Coldharbour
Uffculme, Devon, EX15 3EE

Burnham Nurseries Ltd
(Orchid Paradise)
Forches Cross
Newton Abbot
Devon, TQ12 6PZ
tel. 01626 352233

F.M.M. [FMM]
Unit 5, Kings Park Ind. Estate
Primrose Hill, Kings Langley
Herts., WD4 8ST
tel. 01923 268 699
fax. 01923 261 226
clements@f-m-m.demon.co.uk

Guy Paul & Co. Ltd
Unit B4, Foundry Way
Little End Road, Eaton Socon
Cambs. PE19 3JH

Hawthorn Hill [HH]
12 High Street
Knutton
Newcastle under Lyme
Staffs, ST5 6DN
tel. 01782 623111

Holly Products [HP]
Holly Cottage, Hassall Green
Cheshire, CW11 4YA
tel./fax. 01270 761 403

Cornish Cakeboards
Garth-an-deys
Rose Hill
Goonhavern
Truro, Cornwall, TR4 9JT
tel. 01872 572548

Orchard Products [OP]
51 Hallyburton Road
Hove, East Sussex, BN3 7GP
tel. 01273 419 418

Wyld Court Living Rain Forest
Hampstead Norreys
Berkshire, RG18 0TN
tel. 01635 202444

P.M.E. Sugarcraft [PME]
Brember Road, South Harrow
Middlesex, HA2 8UN
tel. 020 8864 0888
www.pmeltd.co.uk

Renshaw Scott Ltd
Crown Street
Liverpool, L8 7RF
tel. 0151 706 8200
Suppliers of Renshaw's
Regalice sugarpaste
used throughout the book

W. Robertson (Billy's Blocks)
The Brambles, Ryton
Tyne and Wear, NE40 3AN
tel. 0191 413 8144

Squires Kitchen [SK]
Squires House
3 Waverley Lane
Farnham
Surrey, GU9 8BB
tel. 01252 711 749

Sugarflair (food colours)
Brunel Road
Manor Trading Estate
Benfleet, Essex, SS7 4PS
tel. 01268 752 891

The British Sugarcraft Guild
Wellington House
Messeter Place
Eltham, London, SE9 5DP
tel. 0208 859 6943

The Flower Studio
18 The Buttermarket
Thame, Oxon, OX9 3EP
tel. 0184 426 0236

The Old Bakery (Sunrise wires)
Kingston St Mary
Taunton, Somerset, TA2 8HW
tel. 01823 451205

The Porcelaina Society
46 Meadow Way, Tottington
Bury, Lancs., B18 3HU

The Secret Garden (florists)
Clayton Road, Jesmond
Tyne and Wear
tel. 0191 281 7753

Tinkertech Two [TT]
40 Langdon Road, Parkstone
Poole, Dorset, BH14 9EH
tel. 01202 738 049

Wilton [W]
Knightsbridge Bakeware Centre Ltd
Chadwell Heath Lane
Romford, Essex, RM6 4NP
tel. 020 8590 5959
www.cakedecoration.co.uk

Non-UK
Cakes & Co.
25 Rock Hill, Blackrock
Co. Dublin, Ireland
tel. + 353 1 283 6544

Cupid's Cake Decorations
2/90 Belford Street Broadmeadow
NSW 2292, Australia
tel. +61 2 4962 1884

Cake Decorating School of Australia
Shop 7, Port Phillip Arcade
232 Flinders Street
Melbourne, VIC 3000
tel. +61 3 9654 5335

Beryl's Cake Decorating
& Pastry Supplies
P.O. Box 1584
N. Springfield
VA22151–0584, USA
tel. + 1 800 488 2749

International Sugar Art Collection
6060 McDonough Drive
Suite D, Norcross
GA 30093, USA
tel. + 1 770 453 9449

Creative Cutters
561 Edward Avenue, Unit 1
Richmond Hill
Ontario L4C 9W6
tel. +1 905 883 5638

First published in 2002 by
Merehurst, an imprint of Murdoch
Books UK Ltd
Copyright © 2002 Murdoch Books
UK Ltd
ISBN 978-1-90399-215-9

A catalogue record for this book is
available from the British Library.

Commissioning/Project Editor:
Barbara Croxford
Designer: Shahid Mahmood
Design Manager: Sarah Rock
Photographer: Sue Atkinson

CEO: Robert Oerton
Publisher: Catie Ziller
Production Manager:
Lucy Byrne
Sales and Marketing Director:
Andrew McGhie

Colour separation by Colourscan,
Singapore
Printed in Singapore by Tien Wah
Press

Murdoch Books UK Ltd
Ferry House, 51–57 Lacy Road
Putney, London, SW15 1PR
Tel: +44 (0)20 8355 1480
Fax: +44 (0)20 8355 1499
Murdoch Books UK Ltd is a
subsidiary of
Murdoch Magazines Pty Ltd.

UK Distribution
MacMillan Distribution Ltd
Houndsmill, Brunell Road
Basingstoke, Hants RG1 6XS
United Kingdom
Tel: +44 (0)1256 302 707
Fax: +44 (0) 1256 351 437
http://www.macmillan-mdl.co.uk

Murdoch Books®
GPO Box 1203, Sydney
NSW 1045, Australia
Tel: +61 (0)2 8220 2000
Fax: +61 (0)2 8220 2020
Murdoch Books® is a trademark of
Murdoch Magazines Pty Ltd.

Index